THE LIFE SUMMIT

MAP OUT THE LIFE OF YOUR DREAMS IN 6 EASY STEPS

Tim Levy

The Life Summit
Map Out The Life Of Your Dreams In 6 Easy Steps

ISBN 978-1-60037-694-8

Library of Congress Control Number: 2009934403

MORGAN · JAMES
THE ENTREPRENEURIAL PUBLISHER

Morgan James Publishing, LLC
1225 Franklin Ave., STE 325
Garden City, NY 11530-1693
Toll Free 800-485-4943
www.MorganJamesPublishing.com

In an effort to support local communities, raise awareness and funds, Morgan James Publishing donates one percent of all book sales for the life of each book to Habitat for Humanity. Get involved today, visit **www.HelpHabitatForHumanity.org**.

Dedication

To the newest member of our family Isabella Scarlet, who is just two weeks old as we go to press with this book.

Foreword

There are some experiences in life that are *'good, nice, lovely,'* and there are others that are *'great, remarkable, and transformational.'* Being asked to write a few words about Tim Levy and The Life Summit process he presents In this book is definitely an opportunity for me to talk about that second group of experiences…the ones that are amazing, revelatory, and life-changing.

In most books, the foreword is intended to be a persuasive declaration to convince you that, "This book can *change your life!"* Therefore, it has become a rule of thumb that someone – often someone like me (and by that I mean someone who is a complete and total stranger to you) – shares his or her thoughts about how gifted the author is and how great the book is.

I'll be honest. I don't like to follow 'the rules.' So I want to take a departure from the rules and do something radical here…, something I hope will be more meaningful to *you* - the smart, well-read reader. I would like to invite you to simply flick through the following pages, digest some of the easy wisdom at a quick glance, inhale it like a sweet smelling flower…*and let your intuition guide you.*

I'd like you to do what feels *true for you* and act upon that inner-certainty that just knows when something is right. And in taking away the sales pitch here and letting this be simply a moment for your inner reflection, I believe that for some of you, The Life Summit will call to you immediately. For others, The Life Summit will be your constant companion, stalking you until you are ready to surrender to its magnificence.

And this is why, rather than try and convince you that this book will change your life, I believe you will discover that for yourself. The Life Summit simply *is* life-changing as is the sheer intensity of its author.

Tim came into my life through synchronicity and changed my life through mastery. He is a capital-G 'Genius' in real terms, not just because he is smart or clever or intellectual. He is all of those things, most assuredly, but what distinguishes him is his honesty, warmth, and humanity… and unending passion for the process which is 'The Life Summit'. Tim has a zeal in him that burns like a house afire, and the heat…the passion…is contagious. It is simply impossible not to like Tim, even if you really wanted to. He is just that beautiful a person… capital-B 'Beautiful.'

I imagine that many of Tim's readers choose this book searching for a tool, a key, or a masterplan that will reveal to you the brilliance of your life. The Life Summit does that for you, but it goes beyond showing you what's possible and helps you actually grab the 'brass ring' - guaranteed! I have experienced the process intimately with Tim and although I am a coach of a similar style and have authored life-transforming books myself, Tim was able to show me new ways to look at my life.

Maybe it was the process, maybe it was Tim, but I do believe that the combination of the two increased the Genius of it all exponentially. Every day since I have had Tim in my life, it simply has transformed everything – and taken me to another level as well.

Be forewarned. For those of you who are ready to explore the Summit of your life, you must be prepared for the outcome. So know this: if you have challenges in your life that have stopped you in the past, *they will go away.* If you have a dream that hasn't been fulfilled, *it will now happen.* If you have wanted to be a success and have failed, *this is now your time.*

Yes, these are all warnings for something that is just now coming into focus on the horizon. No everyone can see it. But with The Life Summit, it's easy to see a bright future ahead of you. So grab your sunglasses!

The time has come for you to step into the spotlight of your own perfection. To allow your life to unfold, revealing layer after layer of happiness. With Tim to guide you, you will now move up from the midpoint on your 'happiness scale'…inching the needle past 'nice,' 'good,' and 'lovely.' In literally a matter of moments, as you begin to read, you'll be entering a whole new level of being, where words like 'amazing' and phrases like 'Exactly what I wished for' are the status quo.

Congratulations. You don't know it yet. But you're already exactly where you need to be. I applaud you … simply, honestly, whole-heartedly … I applaud you.

Maria Elita
Author 'The NAKED Entrepreneur'
www.MariaElita.com

Table of Contents

Preface

Here's how it happened...

I started off, and I'm getting ahead of myself here, by using the Life Summit process on this very book. I went through the process, step by step, of mapping out the details of my desires for the creation, publishing, marketing and distribution of this book.

Some very specific things popped up for me. I wanted an international publishing deal. I wanted to be able to contribute to and share control in the marketing and distribution of the book. I wanted to help as many people as possible with what I genuinely believe to be a breakthrough process that I've lived and breathed successfully for the past decade or two.

Of course, I didn't have any idea about how I was going to make this happen. Luckily, that was not my job. All I needed to do was get clear about what I wanted...and things started to happen. Things came to me in what seemed to be a mysterious and inexplicable fashion. But *was* there an explanation? I began to wonder if there might be something more to this than meets the eye, more to this amazing sequence of events *than mere coincidence.*

I'll begin at the beginning...

Firstly, I received an out-of-the-blue phone call from a friend of mine in the States who wanted to visit for a month or so. Joseph is one of my closest friends, a truly aligned soul and a model houseguest too. He is great with our children, takes the time to help with the chores and cooks a mean plate of just about anything. So I had just one reaction: Fantastic!

Joseph is also very social, so we went out on the town to an event I'd never have gone to on my own; something called *Couch Surfing.* Couch Surfing is an international online community of travelers who stay on each other's couches as they travel the globe. We met a bunch of them on our night out including a lovely traveler from Los Angeles named Sheila.

Things were already unfolding for me. Can you see it? I couldn't see it, but I felt it. It's precisely these sorts of amazing events that give me that little tingle, that little signature itch that lets me know that the Law of Attraction is 'in the house,' at work, and orchestrating things in response to my desire. It's the best feeling in the world.

Could I have predicted what was happening, or about to happen? No. I don't have ESP. I can't look into the future. Could I have *planned* it out, with an option for each contingency, meticulous in detail? No. I'm an Average Joe...or I guess 'Average Tim' is more accurate. I'm just an everyday guy. I can't control anything in the world with 100% certainty, let alone the details of my own life. It's quite the relief to acknowledge that and to *let it go.* But we'll get to that later.

Let's get back to the story. Events were unfolding, each in its own way taking me a little step towards my desire. I ran into Sheila again when she visited Joseph at my home a week or so later. This was the same day that the first prototype copies of this very book, fresh and crisp from blurb.com, arrived on my doorstep. Sheila happened to be watching as I tore into the package and in response to her request; I agreed to lend her a copy for 24 hrs, no more. I was feeling very protective. After all, these were my very first copies fresh off the press!

Twenty-four hours turned out to be all the time Sheila needed. She emailed this message to me the following day:

'I stayed up all night last Sunday to finish it and I am blown away. Thank you so much for letting me borrow a copy. It is the exact blueprint I need to take me to the next level in my ability to manifest what I want. The book is brilliant and is unlike anything I have encountered.'

Now do you begin to see a shape taking place, a tapestry slowly coming together thread by thread? A few days later, Sheila and I spent close to four hours together actually running the Life Summit process. This was Sheila's comment when we were through:

'I wanted to thank you from the bottom of my heart for going thru the Life Summit process with me. I am still speechless at how you were able to hone in on the exact 2 areas I was completely stuck in!'

She continued…

"I have gone thru The Life Summit process and it is life altering. Can't wait to implement and share my results with the world. Thanks Tim!!"

This was good news; great news in fact. There's nothing like positive feedback to make an author feel good. But what was downright amazing isn't what Sheila said, but what she did. She got in touch with her friend David who owns and runs one of the most progressive publishing houses in the world. It's one of the few businesses that has continued to expand despite the recent economic recession.

Sheila set the stage, and David and I connected briefly via Facebook. He asked me to submit my manuscript via their usual process, which I did immediately. Why the hurry? I was eager, but just as importantly, I was off on holidays with my wife and needed to wrap everything up before our departure. A month later I was back in town starting to pitch various publishers with the intention of getting back in touch with David's Morgan James Publishing as best I could.

The rest, as the saying goes, is history.

Morgan James, the first publisher I sent the manuscript to, picked up the worldwide rights for the book. That's desire number one right there – an international publishing deal. It turns out that Morgan James Publishing not only encourages author participation; they insist on it. That's desire number two right there – the chance to actively participate in and share control in the marketing and distribution of the book. And desire number three, my desire to help as many people as possible? Well that's where you come in.

My greatest desires for this book have come true thanks to *the very process described in the book itself!* Not that I needed any more evidence that this process works. I had already used it to get an ideal wife, awesome kids, my children's books published, nationally touring stage shows, my own network broadcast TV show... Need I go on? My dreams have all come true and my desires have all been made real in ways I could never have imagined, let alone forced into reality simply by my own efforts. In fact, when I lean back, get out of the way and let events unfold focusing solely on *what I want* rather than *how to get it*, the reality has turned out *even better* than my dreams. I love that...

...and I'd love for you to have the same experience in your life. It's the reason I wrote this book and am working on its soon-to-be-published sequels.

My Path to This Place

You can't get anywhere unless you know where you're going. Where is this book taking you?

You know, I can't get my fill of the Law of Attraction. I've always loved it and always will. Whether I'm watching 'The Secret,' reading the works of other proponents of the Law of Attraction like Wallace Wattles, Robert Collier, and Helena Blavatsky, who all published books in the early 1900's; or soaking up information from contemporary luminaries like Wayne Dyer and Deepak Chopra, I always come away with more and more 'golden nuggets' from this clearly enlightened material. I was privileged to meet Deepak one day, and boy, that guy is smart! It comes off him in waves.

The one thing that annoyed me about much of what some people call the New Age approach is that it didn't seem very much 'of the real world'. It's all very 'higher plain,' very *theoretical*...and ungrounded. It feels impractical to methodical, left-brained, business-oriented minds like mine. I'm all about tangible results not wishy-washy stuff! How about you?

Most of the material I've seen on the Law of Attraction simply reports that this is a process by which you make things 'come to you.' Well okay. That sounds great. How does it work is what I wanted know.

Are you cruising along in your rusty old car thinking, 'I wish I had a new Porsche,' and suddenly a new one drops out of the sky? Apparently for those who are truly enlightened by the Law of Attraction, it just might happen that way. For me, your quintessential Average Joe, it doesn't.

Is the Law of Attraction all about positive affirmations? Are you meant to dedicate the waking moments of your day to a zombie-like repetition of, 'I want more money, I want more money, I want more money' until it is delivered to your door by means of a friendly postal delivery worker?

Just as I'm sure you do, I wanted to know the sure fire, happens-every-time, tried-and-true, *proven* way to work with the Law of Attraction in everyday life. I'm talking about the kind of everyday life those of us in the real world are living. We're not spiritual yogis wrapped in blankets on a mountaintop in Tibet. We're holding down jobs, juggling work and family, trying to raise kids, making monthly car payments and carrying a mortgage. You know - *real life*. What works for *that?*

I don't want impractical theory. What I want is a practical, grounded, everyday action plan for living the Law of Attraction. Something consistent with everything I already know from my years in business about planning, implementation and results. I want a clearly defined practice, a process that will consistently keep this way of thinking front-and-center in my mind. I want a way to incorporate these elegant principles into my everyday life with ease.

The First Bricks
Somewhere in the mid-nineties I started to build such a system, blending the fantastic spiritual principles of the Law of Attraction with the practical, business-oriented systems that I'd learned running companies over the years.

And so I worked, over time, at manifesting this process I so desired. I figured it out for myself, and then tried it out on friends and client businesses. Little by little, it started to take shape and finally, coalesced into a consistent form. I diligently polished and refined it until I had something reliable that worked without fail.

I wanted to be practical, not theoretical. I wanted to find out exactly how people were really making the Law of Attraction work for them in their everyday lives.

I wanted to answer questions like:

- How do these principles work when the rubber meets the road?

- What sorts of problems do you come up against, and how can you get past them?

- Does the Law of Attraction make a difference or is it just more new age hokum?

- Does the Law of Attraction heal lives and bodies, making people happier and more enlightened?

- Or does the Law of Attraction just make people frustrated as they try to stay faithful to the principles but find that they cannot?

I imagine these may be some of the questions you're asking as well. If they are; I'm delighted! I think questions are the sign of a lively, inquisitive mind. If you're asking questions like the ones above, then it tells me that you're sharp enough to be **skeptical, but not cynical** and that you're open to the wonderful possibility that this Law of Attraction thing might really be 'it.'

We're in this together...for the long haul. So let's not be strangers! There's nothing I love better than a story with a happy ending, and I'd like to hear yours. Please visit www.thelifesummit.com and send me a note about how this is all working for you. I'd love to hear from you.

For now, however, I'm going to get out of your way and leave you to read. The concepts and processes revealed on these pages have worked for me and they're going to work for you. So please enjoy this book and the life of abundance it makes possible.

I wish you to have the *very life of your dreams*.

Yours in life,

Tim Levy

September 2009

Welcome to Life at the Top

Do you belong here? Is The Life Summit for you? Yes! This book *was written for anyone who wants a better life and wants to know the best way to get it.*

The Life Summit is for people who want to get more clarity on what they desire and to attract those things into their lives. It's for men and women of all ages who feel dissatisfied with where they are now and want to take conscious steps to improve their lot in life.

Now while I'm guessing **I've pretty much described everyone except infants,** here are some of the people who have joined me in successfully using the Life Summit process over the past few years.

- **Dean** is an Internet professional working from the West Coast of the U.S. He's in his mid-thirties, based in a beautiful home nestled in the woods in Oregon.

- **Desiree** is a twenty-something professional designer and recent mom who makes her home in London in the United Kingdom.

- **Mariah** is a thirty-something, hot-shot, jet-setting executive for Soul Coach based on the east coast of Australia. She travels the world promoting her books.

- **Dave** is a forty-something real-estate entrepreneur based on the East Coast of America. He is recovering from a series of medical issues that have crept up on him over the last few years. He is looking to adapt his world view from living an outdoor adventurer's life to living an outdoor adventurer's life...with the physical challenges.

- **Sheila** is a forty-something human resources executive out of Los Angeles, California. Over the last six months she has quit her old job, quit her old house, and quit her old life in favor of 'starting fresh,' completely from scratch. She is looking to accelerate her new life plans into abundance and right now!

- **Joseph** is a twenty-something rock-star in the making. Based originally on the West Coast of America, he has been touring across Europe, the United Kingdom, and Australia almost constantly for the last eight years. He is looking for some definition and drive around the launch of his next album and the tour that accompanies it.

These, then, are the kinds of people that are using the Life Summit process *right now*. You might see a little of yourself in them, and you might see a little more of yourself throughout the book, as we use the real life examples from their lives and mine to illustrate the process.

You'll notice that most of them, having gone through the process, are actively pursuing their dreams. They're also pretty normal, practical and sometimes gently spiritual people with one particular difference.

They've decided that they want more in life than the standard job, the standard car and the standard house. They're reaching for higher levels of relationships, high levels of abundance and higher levels of satisfaction.

The Life Summit is the tool they've chosen to get them there.

Understanding The Life Summit

So just what *is* The Life Summit, anyway? The Life Summit is a process of thinking and doing that is designed to bring consistent, unambiguous focus to your desires, thus leveraging the Law of Attraction into your everyday life in a practical way.

Not familiar with the Law of Attraction yet? Don't worry. Learning about it is all part of the fun. And it will be fun!

The Life Summit process releases the imaginative power of your creative, spiritual, artistic side, and then the logical power of your organized, practical, scientific side.

> ### A Note on Left Brain vs. Right Brain
> A quick little note here on left and right brain. While I'm sure most of you are already familiar with this terminology, here's what I mean by it.
>
> The 'right brain' is mainly creative and intuitive while the 'left brain' is all about reasoning and problem-solving by the numbers. We go into more detail in the next chapter.
>
> It is when these two powerful internal resources work together -- harmoniously and in careful sequence (but never simultaneously) -- that you become the most powerful manifestor that you can be.

Manifestor? If you just rushed over to look for this word in the dictionary, it isn't there. But I don't think we need Daniel Webster to explain it. A 'manifestor' is someone who is adept at bringing their dreams into reality; someone who is *manifesting* their desires **as actual, tangible events**. It's the process of bringing something ethereal, such as an idea or desire, into the real, physical world.

In some traditions, there are individuals who become so good at this -- prophets, gurus, yogis and spiritual leaders, for example – that they are said to be able to manifest objects instantly.

But first, here's what I know you're on the edge of your seat waiting for, saying to yourself, "Come on, Tim! Get to it. I want to start my journey".

Outlining Your Journey

I always like to know where I'm going before I begin, so let me give you an overview of the road ahead, with all the stops you'll make along the way…and even a 'sneak peek' at your destination!

- **Go to Your Happy Place Space** – First you'll learn how to get yourself into a creative, positive state in a creative, supportive environment

- **Surround Yourself With Everything You Need** – Next, you'll equip yourself with all the right materials, right people and right amount of time to work uninterrupted for a few hours or maybe even a day

- **Check Logic at the Door** – This is where things really get going! I'll show you how to banish your left brain completely from the room, entertaining only the limitless, creative, fun, funny right brain side to dream up your ideal life, to dwell upon your long term desires. You'll engage in a process known as **Mind Mapping** with the help of people who are there for you in a non-judgmental and exclusively supportive role.

- **Give Yourself a Break** – You'll take time to turn off the 'machine' and take a breather. Have a bite. Visit the 'necessary.'

- **Invite Logic Back to the Table** – This is another pivotal moment. You'll invite your left brain, the logical part of you that's been locked out of the process, to join you at 'the table' while you usher your right brain out a discreet back door.

- **Throw Down Your Glove** - You challenge your left brain to convert your creative right-brain plan into business, into math, into an empirical, quantifiable plan.

- **Put It On Paper** - You work on paper, transforming all your ideas from thought form into physical word form. You create a series of plans ranging from the long to the medium to the short term.

- **Get In Training** – Begin weekly or daily 'workout' sessions designed to manufacture these clearly planned desires into consistent, unambiguous, focused thoughts.

- **Walk the Talk** - Now you live the Life Summit process to leverage the Law of Attraction in your life in a practical, daily way. You leap into living with new joy, detachment, zest and excitement. You charge into your day with firm and clear expectations of leading a wonderful life. And you watch as your desires manifest in their own, unique, amusing and unanticipated ways.

*Next, we'll look into a set of tools that you're going to need for the Life Summit process. These tools are **facilitating, brainstorming and mind mapping**.*

Your Life Summit Tool Kit

The Life Summit process is all about searching your soul to bring your true desires into consciousness. I won't lie to you: figuring out what's going on inside yourself is definitely not easy. It's very difficult to be that honest with yourself. So why not get a little bit of help?

Life Summit Tool #1 - Facilitators

Now maybe I'm just a softie, lacking that discipline we spoke about in earlier chapters, but I find it's much more effective to do the Life Summit *with a buddy*. It's certainly more fun!

Now let's just be clear; while you can certainly do the Life Summit process alone, (and I have many times, mainly because my friends/family/wife get bored with me asking to do it all the time) I enjoy it more with a *talented facilitator*.

This doesn't need to be a formal, trained 'Life Summit' facilitator. It can be a friend or a member of your family. Although if you're really stuck, a 'pro' may be just what you need to get un-stuck.

Your Facilitator

I've been blessed with several close friends who now understand and practice this process. We help one another do the work by splitting sessions (half for your partner, half for you) or doing the summit over several days.

By the way, **going somewhere** can be a good idea in that it removes all other distractions. We sometimes go crazy and travel somewhere nice for a few days, maybe even a week, to really get into it. I've traveled everywhere from Magnetic Island to the forests of Italy to do this process.

The Role of a 'Life Summit' Facilitator

Whether you have a friend or family member as your facilitator, it's important that the person you choose understands his/her *role* in the process.

It takes a certain kind of person and personality to help you with your Life Summit because the facilitator's role is so specific. They help get the material out of your head, usually spending some tricky time making your subconscious conscious. If that's what they're doing, then they're facilitating.

The role of the facilitator is to *get the best out of you*. Period.

Facilitators are not there to judge. They're not there to offer opinions. They're definitely not to offer ideas or solutions *unless explicitly asked for*. Your facilitating sidekick is a facilitator only, no coaching allowed, thank you very much.

So I don't do this with my wife.

Actually, strike that. My wife won't do this with me! I'd love to help her through the process and I'd be delighted to share my Summit with her, but we're a little too close. It's nearly impossible for the 'without judgement' thing to happen. Surely you've encountered this with your spouse, best friend, or other loved one.

When I say, 'Darling, my true dream is to quit my boring, dead-end job to be a rock star', she can't just write it on my life map. My dream is just too big in its implications for her life. So she has to pull me down to earth with a judgement, a comment, or a quip, like 'But what about the kids?' or 'Can we really afford to do that?'

As you can imagine, when we're talking about desire, we're talking limitless, creative thinking and massive dreams. We're not interested in reality at this point. This is not the time to focus on 'what is.'

Choosing a 'Life Summit' Facilitator

It's best to pick someone who is close enough to give you some of their time, but not so close as to have their lives inextricably intertwined with your own. That way they can be 'judgement-free' as you express your desire to steal Hugh Jackman away from his current wife or appropriate all the gold locked up tight at Fort Knox.

I've played the role of facilitator dozens of times in business and personal life. I've helped friends evolve their personal plans, facilitated large staff groups in forming the plans for multinational corporations and everything in between.

It's great fun as long as you remember that the facilitator's job is to draw out the other person's desires *without undue comment*. So pick someone who will be able to stick to that role.

It's also nice to have a facilitator who doesn't mind doing the 'grunt work': providing the snacks, keeping loose track of time, and other housekeeping-type chores. That kind of thing is helpful. Also, see if you can find a facilitator who is a whiz with mind maps (we go into them in a moment), someone who will be able to help you take the notes and make the diagrams that you're going to need.

Other than that, the facilitator is to keep his or her eyes on the prize (you and your desires) and their judgments, thoughts and comments strictly to themselves! This is about YOU!

Most of the time you can have your facilitator learn their role as they go. It's not too tricky. And once you have your facilitator sorted out, or perhaps you've decided to go it on your own, you're up to the next step: *understanding brainstorming.*

Life Summit Tool #2 - Brainstorms

Brainstorming is to innovation what baseball is to sports (or football if you're an NFL fan). It's the engine in the car, the wings on the plane, and the genius in the invention. And yet, most of the time, brainstorming is done badly.

So let me whip you through the brainstorming process as I understand it. I'll give you the process as I know it, along with some notes on how to prepare and how it works. I've also included a few tips on what not to do!

And please, even if you're a brainstorming professional, please read this through. There might even be something new to you! And even if it's information with which you're familiar, reviewing it can't hurt.

The Inner Child

Unleashing the inner child, also known as the right brain, is the essence of brainstorming. I'm sure you can remember the lateral bursts of inspiration that came to you so easily as a child, those same bursts that come increasingly rarely now, as an adult, arguably when you need them the most.

Right brain flashes of inspiration as a child include:

- That poetic moment when you decided that the only way to experience a hill was to roll down it.
- That flash of inspiration when you decided that the only way to put toothpaste onto a brush was by using the whole tube.
- That instant when you decided that the most fun to be had on a bridge was to jump off it into the water, regardless of the unchecked torrent that raged below.

The 'What if?' for kids has no limits, no criteria, no safety checks or logic. There is no reason in imagination, and nor should there be. That's what makes kids so great.

Reason is the domain of the inner child's arch-nemesis, the inner adult…also known as the left-brain.

A basic law of physics is that two things cannot occupy the same space at the same time. And these two parts of you should not, under any circumstances, be in the same 'room' in your head at the same time or they will cancel one another out to a large extent. The logical left brain undermines the creative right brain with comments like 'Oh really? And how would that *work?*' or 'It'll never happen' or, 'That's impossible'. These kinds of comments shut the right brain down, leaving your inner child shaking and shivering and curled up in the corner in a fetal position.

In terms of strength, your right-brain is the 90-lb. weakling compared to your left-brain. Logic is powerful, so your left-brain has a million tricks up its mental sleeve that will completely shut down your right-brain function. That's why the Life Summit process is structured so that you hear from each of them separately.

These two aspects of your brain can leave notes for one another to be collected at a later date, sure. No problem. After all, a good inner child ignores all notes with the same passion that the inner adult writes them.

Brainstorming, then, is the domain of your right brain, your super-creative inner child. This little field guide is here to help you bring your *inner child out*. The inner adult can wait, because adults are more patient than children, and be secure in the knowledge that the next chapters are written exclusively for the grown-up in you.

Do's and Don'ts

Over the years, I've found that brainstorming is a kind of ritual. In the same way that the Dalai Lama lights a few candles before he meditates to facilitate the right mental and emotional state, we need to get a few things set up to brainstorm.

First, have a think about **where** you're going to do this. Ideally you should do it in a space you don't use every day. For example, your bedroom isn't good. Nor is your grey work cubicle, regardless of how nicely it's decorated with pictures of your friends and family. The standard boardroom can work, although you might want to move things around a little to give it a different feel. Just make sure that the space doesn't feel normal. It has to feel creative, unusual, new and different!

In my recent past, doing this as a consultant, I've had great success by hiring out a creative brainstorming facility for the day or weekend. These facilities tend to be brightly colored and furnished with huge comfy cushions, lounge chairs and fluorescent bean bags. They also come with snacks, meals and drinks on-call, as well as enough butcher's paper, colored felt-tip pens and sticky tape to decorate the decks of an aircraft carrier. That's good because you're going to need about that much.

If you're doing a Life Summit at home, the 'minimum requirements' are some free wall space and a couch from which you can easily see this space. Tables are less important since we use the walls or available windows/sliding doors instead of horizontal surfaces. My own home brainstorming center is just my home office with a 6x24-foot patch of exposed dry-wall and a bright blue couch set opposite.

Bright colors work, by the way, since they tend to remind you of your childhood.

The most important barometer is the way you feel. Do you feel creative, enlivened and possibly even enlightened in this space? If not, find another or change the one you're in until it inspires you. This place must feel fun, comfortable and safe. You're creating the ideal place to bounce crazy ideas around without judgement or recourse.

What Not to Bring
Imagine you're about to go deep diving in a submarine on war games for the next few hours. This work requires your absolute and undivided attention, so any contact with the outside world is completely banned.

The Banned List
> There will be no mobile or cellular phones
> There will be no local land phones
> There will be no Skype connections, laptops, buzzing, ringing or alarms of any kind
> There will be no access to any communication with anyone, including email and semaphore (i.e. being able to see a

colleague signal you in one corner of the window or via strategic reflection)

You should even do your best to isolate yourselves acoustically, which is to say, make it quiet. If you're in an office with other people working nearby, let them know you're in session and could they please courteously be quiet. If there's loud music nearby, do your best to turn it off.

And of course, let any colleagues, neighbours, pet animals and children know that they're not to interrupt you for any reason, including that stuff that happens when your five year old misses the bowl.

In short, we want an isolation booth of some kind sort of like the cone of silence in Maxwell Smart, only nicer. And if I hear about any violations I'll come around and punish you myself, as local laws allow.

If your inner adult is 'listening in' right now and freaking out about being cut off ("What if something happens?!"), ask it to take a breath. You're not a prisoner. You'll be able to take bathroom breaks and check your cellphone for messages at regular intervals.

Brain Food

If brainstorming is all about the inner child then brainstorming *food* has got to be pretty juvenile too.

The way I think of it is this; what was I eating when I was the most creative? The answer (and this is easy logic) is the food I ate as a child. No, I'm not talking about the over-boiled carrots and ever-so-healthy, ever-so-gross chicken liver pâté.

I mean the good stuff. The party food. You know – when you're running around, crazy with ideas and intentions. Pretty much anything that is bright red or bright blue. I'm talking about the sugar.

When I think of kids' food I see large portions of chocolate in bright cheerful packets. For me these include Hershey's Kisses, Coca-cola, big bags of M&Ms and ice-cream. And hey - no alcohol; anything that dulls the mind is counter-productive.

Borrow $20.00 from the nearest responsible adult (or well-heeled youngster) and get yourself to the candy aisle in the local supermarket. Then go nuts. *Just the act of buying the candy is a kick.* When did you ever have $20.00 to spend this way as a kid?

Feel free to add some useful calories if you must, as the brainstorm can routinely go for hours at a time. I recall my brother and I managing to make a Life Summit session last the better part of a week. So add a few bottles of water, maybe some celery sticks and carrots too. You know—something designed to keep you vertical when the sugar rush from the candy wears off.

Assemble your bounty, put it on a plate and throw it into the middle of the table before you seal the door shut.

Stuff and Nonsense

If you think your Staples rewards card is the best thing in your wallet and your idea of heaven is wandering through the aisles of Office Depot, this step is for you.

Get yourselves to the nearest stationery store, office supply store, big box retailer, office supply cabinet or your child's arts and craft chest and get

- A few dozen sheets of butcher's paper or something else <u>BIG</u>

- Something you can use to stick those pages to the walls, ten a time, without wrecking the paint. (We use Blu-tak, since sticky tape tends to leave gaping holes)

- A few packets of colorful markers, felt-tip pens, crayons and/ or colored pencils. Put them into a big jar or in random bunches around the room. Do not leave them bound up in the packaging. They want to be free and you want to be able to grab them when you need them!

- A few packets of stickers, self-adhesive dots, or Post-It Notes in case you want to mark something as important or, in the event that there is a group, to vote on something

Bring all these things into the space and set them out in a carefully random, messy kind of way. This reflects the random and messy state of most people's brains and certainly the state we want your brains to be in when you brainstorm.

By now, you should have

- A brainstorming space,

- A good chunk of time set aside,

- No communication with the outside world,

- Some good food, and maybe even a bit of fun music,

- A dozen sheets of paper up on the wall, and

- A bunch of creative writing supplies strewn haphazardly

It's time to get into the act.

The Act of Brainstorming

Preparing for brainstorming may take some doing, but the act of brainstorming, itself, is pure simplicity. In essence, it's **asking and answering questions**. All the preparation is designed to get you into the most creative, relaxed and fun state possible, giving your right-brain every permission and incentive to come out and play.

Brainstorming is a mental workout and as with any good exercise, you should warm up first. Any warm up activity is fine as long as it helps you leave your normal concerns behind and get into a relaxed, fun and creative state of mind.

Some people meditate for a bit, some dance; some do a bit of a stretch or aerobics. Some play a game of Monopoly or some Doom on a bunch of networked PCs. Just do *whatever it takes* to get *you* into that critical relaxed, happy and creative state.

One you're in a good state, feeling happy and ready for fun, you can start. Anything goes!

Brainstorming is a random, crazy, fun state in which you're encouraged to break the rules, do things differently and *think outside the box.* While I don't particularly like clichéd phrases like that last one, they're the essence of brainstorming. Brainstorming is being asked to smash all your preconceptions and have fun doing it.

Having said, here are few guidelines:

- Think crazy!
- Think stoopid!
- There are no wrong answers here
- There is no judgment here

Most of us aren't used to this much freedom. So it's wise to actually print those sorts of permissive phrases out and stick them to the walls, just to remind you.

Brainstorm Example

The following is a flow of consciousness example that illustrates a hypothetical brainstorm using a facilitator. Brainstorming on your own is possible, and yet having a facilitator, as we've discussed before, makes things easier and more fun.

For this illustration, imagine you're in a colorful room with lots of space, lots of good food and bright crayons around, facing a wall covered with sheets of empty butcher's paper. Here's how a brainstorm might sound. (*And I've included some notes, 'stage directions' and explanations in italics, too.*)

FACILITATOR: All right, I think we've got everything all set. How are you feeling?

YOU: Pretty good. I'm keen to get into this, but I've never done it before.

FACILITATOR: No problem. I've read the book, I'm clear on how this works, and I'll take you through it. Besides, I've done plenty of brainstorming at work before. I'm an old pro. Just relax and enjoy

(Here the Facilitator is helping you relax, since you want to be in a relaxed and happy state to do your best work. Also she's letting you know that the left brain stuff is taken care of, so you don't have to worry)

YOU: Cool.

FACILITATOR: Before we start do you need a bathroom break or a pick-me-up snack? We've got plenty! What made you choose Twinkies anyway?

YOU: (bashful) You know, I loved them as a kid. I told the checkout person they were for my daughter's birthday party.

FACILITATOR: Did they buy it?

YOU: I don't think so. It didn't help when I ripped the packet open and started munching right there at the counter. I couldn't help myself. I haven't had these in years!

FACILITATOR: I love it! OK. Now today we're going to focus on you and in particular, your vision of your perfect life. In other words we're simply asking *what do you want*, which can really be anything. Then we're going to collect all these things and put them together to create a collage snapshot of your perfect life.

YOU: So you want me to tell you my perfect life?

FACILITATOR: Exactly. Just go for it. What is your perfect life?

                          (Now the Facilitator writes 'perfect life' in the middle of one of the pages on the wall, then circles it, waiting ready for the next thing)

                          (There will likely be a small pause while you gather your thoughts)

YOU: OK, so I want a bright red sports car.

                          (Facilitator leaps into action, notes 'red sports car' on the butcher's paper. Then, she waits, saying nothing at this time, never interrupting the flow)

                          And a million bucks would be good, can I say that?

FACILITATOR: Of course! We're looking for your *perfect* life, not your *half-way perfect* life. There are no rules or judgments here. If you want a million bucks, then I'll put it on the board, no questions asked.

(Facilitator notes down 'a million bucks' on the butcher's paper)

What else?

YOU: I want a great job *(starts to get into a flow)* and a huge bar of chocolate. I want a great new girlfriend and to have awesome sex every night. Can I say that?

FACILITATOR: Remember, no judgement, anything goes. Don't think too much, just keep going! *(continues to make notes on the wall)*

YOU: I want to have lots of time to hang out with my friends. I want ... a trip to Bali and then a trip to Europe. I've always wanted to just cruise Europe for, say, 6 months, with no fixed plans. You know, just drifting.

FACILITATOR: *(filling out the Mind Map...the subject of the next chapter, so just be patient!)* Got it! Keep going.

YOU: OK, good

(At this juncture, you take a moment to go over what is already on the wall, which gives you more ideas)

I've got a million bucks, a great girlfriend and cool holidays. Oh yeah, I also want a big house. With a white fence and a dog and a pool and a nice lawn with plenty of room for the kids to play, you know ... one day.

FACILITATOR: *(just nods, taking notes)*

YOU: And I want to go out twice a week to the coolest night clubs and to that place ... what's it called ... you know, that new place downtown?

FACILITATOR: I'll just write going out—don't worry about the details yet. Just keep telling me all the stuff you want in big, broad strokes.

YOU: That seems like a lot already!

FACILITATOR: Not really! Remember, this is about your perfect life – so fill it up, baby! Can you give me anything else right now?

YOU: I don't know ...

FACILITATOR: OK – no problem. Then let's go back and get a little more specific. I want some juicy details. Tell me more about the red car; what kind is it, for example?

YOU: It's a Ferrari. No, scratch that, it's an Aston Martin DB9. No! It's a Porsche.

FACILITATOR: Why not have them all! I'll just write them all down for now.

YOU: Sweet! OK, three red sports cars, then, and a boat. Maybe it's red too...

… And that's how it goes.

A brainstorm is simply a place to let your thoughts run wild, without the normal filters, terms and conditions that are so limiting in your every day life. It's a flow of questions, answers, daydreams and explorations.

There are no right or wrong answers, there are just *answers* in brainstorming. Remind you of the Law of Attraction at all? Of course it does; they're deeply aligned.

Anyway, let's leave the analysis for later. Analysis with its roots in logic and 'what is' have no place in a brainstorm anyway. For now, just enjoy the dreaming, wax lyrical and let yourself go.

A brainstorm and everything surrounding it are all part of the process of generating a focus, a set of thoughts, words and inspired actions to leverage the Law of Attraction, as discussed in the first part of the book.

And that's how brainstorming works!

You'll notice that I mentioned a specific method of taking notes on the butcher paper called Mind Mapping. It's an organic, associative and usefully parallel method of taking notes in a brainstorm and as such, very useful right about now. Let's have a bit of a look at this in the next chapter.

Life Summit Tool #3 - Mind Mapping

Mind mapping is all about links. Let me tell you more...

It turns out that our brains are made up of loads of little cells all linked together to form a big gooey mess inside our heads. You've probably heard all this before, though possibly expressed more scientifically, and it doesn't really matter except for one point. Our minds are made of links. Links are, by definition, *associative*.

What this means is that the information in our brains is not sequential, with all facts laid out in a particular order like the pages in an encyclopedia. Our minds are more like Google and the Web. They consist of millions of little info-bits all linked together.

When we're trying to remember something or create something in our brains, we throw in a search term, just like searching Google. And, like Google, the mind throws back a bunch of answers related to that query. What's more, Google's answers are linked to further information, further pages and further questions that come up as you progress. Just like the search results in our minds.

Let's say you start by throwing a question into your brain like, 'What kind of shoes would I like to buy?' Instantly, your mind returns a bunch of directly and indirectly associated answers like,

- I like those ones we saw in Vogue; which issue was that?
- I like the ones Neve was wearing at that party; did I book that follow-up lunch with her yet?
- I like blue, but I'm not sure if blue is good for shoes, but didn't we see some like that one time?
- High heels are bad, they're killer, remember that time I got one stuck in a drain?

In other words, everything is *linked*. One question brings many answers from your linked or associative memory. Each of the new details that are brought forth can frequently link into other details until you're daydreaming off on some tangent, quite possibly having forgotten the original question. Sound familiar?

So! Why fight it? Let's go with it. Let's use a form of note-taking which is associative *just like your mind*. Some years ago the brilliant Tony Buzan developed a planning technique. You'll find his best-selling books listed on Google. And what is Tony's brain child?

It's called **Mind Mapping**.

Since we're going to be using it all through the Life Summit process, I've created this section...a rough and ready guide to Mind Mapping... to get you ready for action.

For my money, Mind Mapping is *the* way to get any creative process down on paper.

Of course you can use any technique you want to keep track of your Life Summit. In fact, I encourage you to use whatever works for you! I've simply found through experience that Mind Mapping has worked for me and my clients over the course of years.

What I want you to understand is the result is more meaningful than the process. Whether you use Mind Mapping or another strategy, what matters is that you have a way to take your ideas and get them onto the page quickly and simply. This is your opportunity to get your thoughts into word form and from there into inspired actions. It is this sequence that actives the powerful Law of Attraction to act in your favor.

Just go back to the chapter 'Thought, Word and Deed' if you've forgotten.

Okay...back to Mind Mapping.

As I said, Mind Mapping is all about links. It's also all about creativity and fun (at least for me). That's the reason I like to have strategies that help me tap into childhood when things like desire and imagination were free and easy.

Make Mapping Fun

To bring out the big kid in you, I suggest getting hold of some butcher's paper and tacking it up to the wall. If you can't get or don't like the idea of butcher's paper any **oversize paper** will do. It does need to be big though...*really big*. So you can think big.

There are two reasons I love to tack paper to the wall. As a child, I was always told 'Don't write on the walls,' so this is a fun way to thumb my nose at the rules. It's also a great way to get a broad perspective. It's possible to put a dozen mind maps on the wall and easily see them all at once. If you lay them flat, it's much harder to see them all, thus denying you easy access to the big picture, which we want.

Now, grab some pens. I suggest that you abandon typical, boring work pens and pencils. They're no fun. They're for dreary things. Also, they tend not to work on walls where you have to write with the pen held horizontally as opposed to vertically. Ball point pens, for example, require that the ink flow down by means of gravity and therefore don't work on walls. Unless you have one of those very cool astronaut pens like they featured in an episode of Seinfeld.

For *me* as a Mind Mapper, I prefer to use colorful markers. Around here, we call them Textas. I have a pack of 24; an entire rainbow at my disposal.

Is your left brain worried that what you write in pen is permanent and can't be changed? What if it's wrong?! If you can quiet down your inner adult, you'll remember that you won't need an eraser because in brainstorming there are no wrong ideas...hence nothing to cross out.

When you have

>Big paper up on the wall
>A wide array of colorful markers
>Passion to get started

...you've got everything you need. You're ready to Mind Map.

I'm going to use a topic that is completely unrelated to the Life Summit to demonstrate how Mind Mapping works. It's a topic that's near and dear to my heart: entertaining. Let's say we want to use creative planning for a party, so a Mind Map would be ideal.

Bullseye Your Main Topic

Start the process by putting your topic in the middle of the page. I like to circle it, put it in a bullseye, and I tend to use one color for this. This is *my* approach. I want to remind you again that in Mind Mapping there is no *one* way to commit your thoughts to paper. As long as you can look at it later and understand your own notes and structure then you're doing it right!

Your inner child likes to run free, so there are also no rules with Mind Mapping. These are just **guidelines** to give you a rough idea of how it's done.

So, you're a party animal and right now you should have something on your Mind Map that looks a bit like this.

Create Arms

Now you start to expand the Mind Map in an organic, random, associative kind of way. Just see where your thoughts lead you. Don't try to control them.

Why work like this instead of more methodically? Because, as discussed above, your mind is not methodical. It's organic, random and associative. Oh and hey, let's not forget that random thinking is more fun, too!

When you think 'party' words and phrases will start to come to mind. So you add 'Party Food', and 'Invitations,' and 'Where it's at' to the paper. These things are just pouring out of my head, so I get them written down ASAP to keep the flow going.

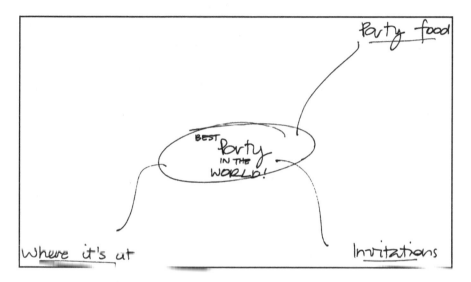

Sometimes I underline each of these significant topics and use 'arms' to connect them back to the main topic in the middle to represent that they are linked. There are no rules about the connecting line; it can be straight, squiggly or a series of precision dots.

Free Associate to Create Links

At this point you've probably noticed that other ideas relating to the topics connected by the arms are crowding into your mind...ideas that are **linked** to the topics you've just written down, and just as eager to join the party, so to speak.

Under 'Party Food' for example, I immediately think of 'Chocolate Cake', 'Cocktail Weenies' and 'Napkins'. It doesn't matter that 'napkins' aren't a food (unless you're a naughty puppy). This is not an exercise in getting things perfect and right, this is Mind Mapping, Baby, and your mind is a messy place. Well, mine certainly is. Yours too?

Okay, now I'm on a roll and linked, associated thoughts are bursting out of my head. I quickly jot down 'Plastic Plates' and 'Plastic Cutlery' under 'Party Food' then randomly go off into a daydream about this cool party I went to in Cannes last year. Ooh yes, they had stilt walkers and a DJ. I bang them down under a new topic, 'Cool Extra Stuff'. Of course, I have no idea how I'm going to make those things happen or if I can even afford them. But there's nothing to stop me from creating these links. My left brain is completely switched off. Excellent!

Of course, you needn't limit your links to nice, hierarchical ones. Mind Maps are meant to be chaotic, like your brain. You can make random links between any two things, or even links between one thing and several others. It's madness!

All of a sudden I realize that my bullseye topic can be improved. This is no longer just 'a party'. Now it's about making the 'Best Party in the World!' With that in mind, I amend the main topic to read, 'Best Party in the World'.

Now I'm on fire. My Mind Map looks like this.

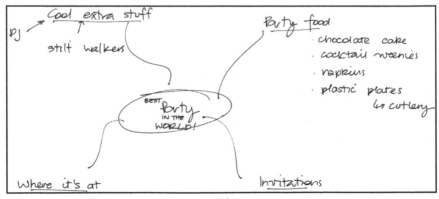

Go 'Crazy' with Ideas

My mind is continuing to churn creatively: if I have stilt walkers and a DJ, then I want my invitation to have pictures of them in it too. Should I do an email invitation or put one in the mail? Can I afford the postage? STOP! I catch myself. That last question is strictly left brain stuff. So I just write both options down under 'Invitations'.

Next, I catch sight of 'Where It's At' and write down 'My Place', then realize that last time I had a party 'chez moi,' the place was trashed. So I go ahead and write down 'Sydney Café' which is a favorite eatery, then 'the local MacDonald's', and finally 'Anywhere except my place' beside that...along with a little 'too messy' comment.

My Mind Map is looking like this.

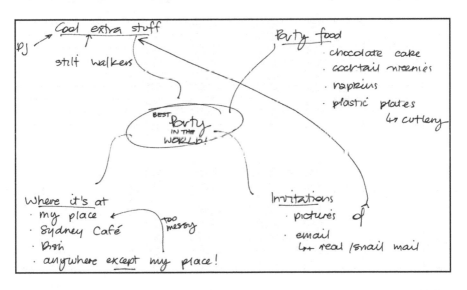

You can see why you'll need such a big piece of paper! I've barely scratched the surface with this Mind Map and could definitely expand it with more arms and links. But I'm sure you get the idea by now.

The Mind Mapping process is a perfect mirror of the Brainstorming process. It's an untidy, hectic and colorful record of all your creative thoughts all on one page and an illustration of the arms and links between them. What's written down isn't evaluated for practicality. We'll figure out the left brain part later. For now, just knowing the Mind Mapping technique is enough.

Mind Mapping with A Facilitator

As you've probably figured out by now, this is not a neat, ordered, professional practice. Mind Mapping is, by design, a messy, jaggy, goofy reflection of what's going on in your brain. So please, don't make it neat. Don't re-write it at the end so 'the boss' (your brain's left side) will think you're perfect. We'll do that later using a process designed to translate this right-brain thing into a left-brain thing. For now, your job is to sit back, kick off your shoes and *relaaaaaaax* your mind into its most creative, free space.

With that in mind, I usually get my facilitating friend to physically fill out the Mind Maps for me. I don't want to even *think* about pens and paper, let alone use them, when I'm in a creative space. When I'm on a roll, I just want to keep rolling. So consider showing your friend this chapter before you start and discussing ways to free yourself to brainstorm without boundaries.

Free Mind Mapping Software

By the way, I should tell you there is plenty of Mind Mapping software online. Feel free to Google it and download the package of your choice. There's a no-cost version called FreeMind, and I'm sure there are many more. I don't use them myself.

My problem with Mind Mapping software is that brainstorming isn't something to do on a computer. It just doesn't get you to the same creative place as crayons and writing on the walls. Computers are inherently left-brained in that they start focusing you on things like font sizes and making sure that things are *exactly right*.

So let me suggest that if you feel you really must use the software to record your thoughts, hold off until *after* you've messed up the walls. That way you get the best of both worlds.

Understanding Desire
and the Law of Attraction

If you've been watching TV, reading books or newspapers, or simply surfing the Internet, then chances are you've heard about the Law of Attraction.

The logic is simple. When you focus your thoughts, words and actions unambiguously and consistently on your dreams, you bring them into reality. Most people, however, fail to do this, and therefore they fail to manifest their dreams. The closest most people come is during a brief moment of clarity around New Year's Day when they announce their 'resolution' to take positive action in their lives. However few follow through with the consistent focus it takes to achieve things.

The process of the Law of Attraction is 'mystical,' but it's also logical. What you focus on, talk about and act consistently on has the best opportunity of becoming real or 'made manifest' in your life. The flip side of the coin is equally logical. What you fail to focus on, talk about or act on will not become real.

That's just the beginning. The Law of Attraction also says that what you focus on, unambiguously and consistently, in fact *must* come to you. That it is *drawn to you* as if you're some kind of magnet. If you're of a more religious bent, then you could say that the Law of Attraction is God's response to prayer. If you're of a more spiritual bent, you might say that the Law of Attraction is a connection to what Deepak Chopra refers to as the Infinite Field. He says that the unlimited organizing power of this field will actually bring the desired circumstances, connections, opportunities and ideas into your life.

Either way, there's something more to this than what you can see with your eyes. Something magical, mystical and fun! Oh – and did I mention the one critical factor? The Law of Attraction really works.

'It really works' is the reason that the Law of Attraction has found believers all over the planet. It has come into mainstream consciousness over the last few years with movies, books and seminars like 'The Secret' and Esther and Jerry Hicks' 'The Teachings of Abraham'. Countless proponents from Wayne Dyer to Oprah are all saying the same thing: that the Law of Attraction is the single most powerful tool of manifestation in the world today.

Is it *really* as simple as that? Almost. Because, in truth, nothing in life is ever truly simple is it? The Law of Attraction brings you what you consciously desire and -- and here's the catch -- what you unconsciously desire. It cuts both ways.

Let's say, for example, that you've got your mind set on having a million dollars. Great. Let's say, however, that what's in your heart is different. Deep down, under the surface, you believe that you don't deserve it.

Or that it'll never happen. Or that you have to work for fifty years to earn that kind of money and you'll still come up short. Those two belief systems are at odds with each other, polar opposites that can completely stalemate your success.

The Law of Attraction isn't judgmental; it's not going to pick and choose between your thoughts, only bringing the positive ones to you. I wish it were that easy! The Law of Attraction, however, is more like gravity. It's implacable. It's mechanical. It's unavoidable. What you believe is what you attract...including the negative.

Let's have a closer look at how this works when you're having an internal conflict.

If you say, 'I want a million dollars,' but simultaneously believe, 'Money is the root of all evil' then you're in internal conflict. If you say, 'I want the perfect man,' but simultaneously believe, 'All the good men are gone', then you've got an idea war on your hands.

Since the Law of Attraction is non-judgmental and simply brings you everything you ask for, it will attempt to bring you both the thing you want and the thing you don't. If these things conflict, then they can cancel each other out, or bring you some kind bizarre, mangled, unsatisfactory hybrid of the two.

Working with the Law of Attraction must include, therefore, a process of improving your **mental discipline**. You must train yourself to be aware of your expressions of conscious desire and aware of unconscious conflicting thoughts until you're like a laser, focusing on your true desire without internal disagreement or ambiguity.

What I mean by mental discipline is that you must become more aware of your thoughts, develop mastery over them so that you eventually are able to choose which thoughts to think and which to discard. Clearly the ideal is to focus exclusively on things you want, releasing all conflicting thoughts forever. This is what I mean by being unambiguous. I mean having the discipline to focus solely on the things you want, rather than the conflicts, doubts or fears that oppose them. Believe me, this is harder than it sounds!

Working with the Law of Attraction requires that you organize your thoughts and focus them into an unambiguous, consistent expression of your desire. Having said that, once you've got this going, once you live this way, it's simply amazing what life brings implacably, mechanically and unavoidably to your door. It's nothing short of everything you truly desire.

As I have followed my desire to implement, then refine this process over nearly two decades, people began to say two things.

First, they became used to me achieving the impossible. They said things like,

- 'Sure you've got a nationally broadcast TV show -', or
- 'Sure you've got a multiple book deal', or
- 'Sure you're going to the south of France to pitch your show to the world!'
- So I knew that the process was working.

Secondly, those who knew I had a process started asking if they could try it out in their lives too, and if I might write it out in book form so that anyone interested could benefit.

So here it is. *The Life Summit*. It's a practical, everyday process that incorporates the profound principles of the Law of Attraction into your lives in a measurable, business-like, daily way. Along the way I worked on this with my brother Nicholas. He was already working in the strategic planning arena professionally for companies in Australia, the UK and further abroad. He was an inspiration and a big help, thanks Nick!

This book helps you figure out your long term dreams and then manifest them. It's a repeatable, easy to understand process that enables you to leverage the Law of Attraction in pursuit of the perfect life. And of course, I've thrown in a few amusing stories from my own real life as I explore what it means to live this process consistently.

Just for the record, there are **two more books underway**. The second book is called 'The Life Summit for Business'. It covers the Life Summit process for businesses and business projects. The third in the series is called 'The Life Summit: Stories from the Road'. It's all about the experience of living 'The Life Summit' every day. So keep your eye out for those books and more. The easiest way to ensure that you're in the loop is to visit my website at www.thelifesummit.com. There's a simple form you can use to opt-in to my subscriber list to be notified of release dates and other Law of Attraction news.

But let's get back to *this* book and *this* moment…and you.

This book, 'The Life Summit', exists to bring you the abundant, happy and enlightened lives that every one of you came here to live.

So let's get into it!

Thought, Word and Deed

OK – so the Law of Attraction brings you what you think about. It's a great theory, but how does that work in real life?

I'm sure we've all heard the phrase 'Thought, Word and Deed'. It's been around, recognized and used, for some thousands of years. Of course, these days we've replaced the word 'deed' with the more current-sounding 'action.'

Whichever way you say it, 'Thought, word and deed' are interconnected. Together they influence the Law of Attraction.

Thought

If you have a thought, then you've taken the first step in attracting that idea into your life...even if you don't realize it.

For example, you might think about a friend, and then soon after, out of the blue, that friend calls. Or maybe you think about a frothy chocolate milkshake, only to have your spouse whip one up for you when you get home, without you even asking! (I love it when that happens; and not just because I'm a pushover for milkshakes.)

And it works both ways, remember? You might go to work thinking 'God, I hope I don't get fired today. The economy is terrible right now and we didn't get that big account recently, so I know I'm on the chopping block.' You get to your desk only to find a pink slip waiting for you...*just as you thought it would.*

Thought is **the first step of manifesting dreams into reality**. Focused thought is a powerful tool on its own. But in the Law of Attraction, it isn't alone. There are other tools and that makes the process work even better. I like to follow 'thought' with the next, even more powerful step...

Word

Words are even more powerful than thoughts for bringing your desires into reality. Words are, obviously, **thoughts in physical form.** Simply by virtue of turning your thoughts into words you are more powerfully manifesting those ideas.

Whether you write your words down on a page in your journal or speak the words aloud in conversation over the phone or in person, you're that much closer to manifesting your dreams.

A Little Thoughts-and-Word Story

This is all very well, talking about the theory, but I promised you practical information. So how does it work in real life? See if this little story rings any bells for you.

Let's say, for a moment that when you were a young person you found yourself dreaming about a season ticket to a top NFL team. Man, oh MAN! You wanted those tickets badly. You could feel those tickets in your hot hand. You could almost taste how good it would feel to go to the ballpark every week, right? Seats nice and close to the action, the smell of fresh cut grass from the field, the sight of those massive players running, sweating and puffing -- you could just feel it. You even became a fan of one particular team, following them in the papers and on TV as best you could. There was nothing you wanted so badly as to go and see every game they played

It was not until you started to use words, however, that it started to really come true. OK sure, nagging your parents might not have been the best possible way to use your words, but boy, it was powerful, right? Even if your parents hated it! All night and day you harassed your parents for the tickets until finally it's your birthday and then WHAMMO! There they were, complete with your very own football for practice in the back yard. There they were, your season tickets, fresh and crisp in your very own hand.

Hey, this stuff really works!

- [ ] **You have a thought**. In this case, you have the desire for season tickets to the football.
- [ ] **You bring those thoughts into word form**. And not just once. You ask your parents for the tickets again and again and again.....*consistently.*

Thoughts and words are a pretty powerful combination. Whether you're an entrepreneur dreaming of a business deal, an eager-to-be-a-bride hoping for a special proposal complete with diamond ring, or a football-loving youngster who wants to see every game of the season, words are a powerful way to bring your dreams into reality.

But if you want to talk about 'power,' nothing is more powerful than...

Deed

Actions (deeds) are the choice, physical tool for manifesting physical things in physical reality. Actions make it happen, right? At least that's what most people think. From the perspective of this book, actions don't 'make it happen'. They're an integral part of an interconnected process that makes things happen (translation: manifests dreams.) We'll talk more about what that means in a moment.

A Note on *Inspired* Actions

Ill-conceived, un-thought-out random actions will not 'Make it Happen'. You have to take the *right* actions. Don't make the rookie mistake of taking action just because you want to be doing *something*. You need to know what you're doing. And in that sense, Nike's motto 'Just Do It' simply does not apply here.

Instead of random actions, what you need to take are *inspired actions*, in a consistent and planned fashion, that ultimately bring your dreams into reality. Here's a real life example that illustrates the concept of inspired actions and how using them changed one man's desire from the stuff of dreams into something tangible.

Anthony Horowitz is an author, screenwriter and film producer. We met when he came on my TV show a year or so back. He wrote the very successful 'Alex Ryder' series, starting with 'Stormbreaker' which was outselling Harry Potter at one time. He told me his story during an interview on my show Groovedelicious and then filled in some more details that same night over dinner.

Anthony started writing books in 1979. It wasn't a 'job' to him. He was inspired to take this action; it was something he just loved to do. The next year and every year thereafter, he released a book without fail and with an unambiguous focus, writing title after title after title. And boy, was he consistent. Anthony released twenty books over *twenty years* in this way. And while they were all published, none of them was a runaway success.

Suddenly, in the year 2000, Anthony became an 'overnight success.' For no apparent reason that he could immediately pinpoint, the Alex Ryder series took off. The Alex Ryder series was selling like hotcakes, so the publisher re-released Anthony's other titles and they became best sellers too! At one point, Anthony's books were in 7 of the top 20 positions in the Children's Book charts. Not bad for someone who 'failed' for 20 years!

Did Anthony 'make it happen?' To the best of his knowledge, no. He just kept writing, taking consistent action doing something he absolutely loved until it took off with its own perfect timing. He was just 'inspired.' And that, of course, is *precisely* what made it happen.

Anthony became so successful that he was able to write and fund a feature film based on the book, starring Mickey Rourke as the villain. The film adaptation of 'Stormbreaker' went to reach number 1 on the

UK charts. When I met Anthony, he was on a worldwide publicity tour promoting the film, and it couldn't have happened to a nicer, more genuine (and genuinely passionate about his film) fellow. He's currently working on the script for the sequel. I'd say his chances for success are excellent, wouldn't you?

Doing vs. Being

Humans have changed through the centuries. People seem to have lost their capacity to just 'be.' Now, I've noticed that there's almost a cultural imperative to 'do'. So many people, especially those chasing a big career, are all about 'doing'. They have outrageous to-do lists crowding their desks. They are constantly in motion, running around madly as they pursue their goals. They start early, work late and presumably collapse in bed at night, only to rise early to do the same thing the following day.

But why? This, in fact, is not the best way to get what you want. It's not even a particularly good way to get what you want, unless you're looking for stress, dysfunction and perhaps a stroke before you're fifty.

If you're *not,* then inspired action is what you need, and to get inspired, you need to 'be,' not 'do.' Take the time to sit, perhaps meditate, and certainly cogitate until an inspired action pops into your head. Get inspired by something you'd love to do, something that is fun for you, something aligned to the unequivocal manifestation of your dreams. You're looking for something that *you actually feel like doing*. **Nothing less will do.** And you'll know that idea for action is an inspired one because you'll be busting to do it, unable to hold back, smiling with anticipation and feeling great about it. In short, you'll be feeling inspired.

So that's the trilogy: thought, word and deed, the three powerful steps of manifestation. You'll see how this trilogy **forms the foundation** of the Life Summit process as the book unfolds.

Desire

If thoughts are so powerful, the starting stage of a sequence that moves into words and actions, then the question is "What should you be thinking about?"

When working with the Law of Attraction, you should consistently focus on what you desire. Desire is one of my favorite words. Why am I such a big fan? Because when you know what you want, what you desire, you are at the beginning point for everything. **Without desire, you have nothing.**

Let me be more specific. If you are carrying focused desires with you as you travel through this life, then you've got a great shot at manifesting those desires. Without them, you live in a world where 'things just happen to you'. Put another way, you either take control of your life by staying focused on your desires, or someone else will take control of it for you and make you an instrument of *their* desires.

The Basics of Desire

So what do I mean by desire? Here are some examples.

- You want a million dollars? That's a desire.

- You want a trendy red bike with all the trimmings? That's a desire.

- You want to have a healthy body, meaningful relationships, a sporty red sports coupe, and lots of time to spend enjoying it all? These are all desires.

Without desires to clarify your path, you're stumbling around in a fog. This is what enlightened gurus refer to as 'sleeping even when you're awake.'

It is desire that brings you everything you want in this world. And why? It is because **desire is the fuel that powers the Law of Attraction.**

Let's take a step back for a moment. Let's take a look at your life. More specifically, let's take a look at what goes on inside your head and what you habitually think about.

Day to day, if you're like most other humans, you wander around in a bit of a blur. Most of what you think one day is very similar to what you think the next; each day generally similar and more or less undistinguished.

Here's a typical 21st Century morning scenario: You wake up and think 'What time is it? Am I early or late?' Then, you jump into the list of things you have to do. Are you looking after kids? Then it's getting them up and dressed. They have to eat the food and clean the teeth. You have to get lunch in a box and send them off to school.

Are you a member of the work force, too? Then the next task is to get yourself washed, dressed, fed and off to work, possibly battling the transport system to get there on time. The list of Things I Should Do, Things I Could Do, and Things I Want to Do gets longer and longer, and it never seems to end.

Maybe your To Do List is 'formal,' with priorities, time codes, and even color codes intended to ensure that everything is done right on schedule. And, if a task is not completed in the allotted time, then you shunt it onto the list for tomorrow, and the day after that, and the day after that. I believe this endless cycle epitomizes that awful human existence know as 'the rat race', the endless hurry and scurry to get things done as you struggle through life with nothing but brief mandated 'rest periods' known as weekends to break up the monotony of all that running. And what do you do on your weekend? You get the chance to catch your breath and recharge your batteries, simply so you can start on your list all over again on Monday.

Surely that's not why we were put on this Earth!

It's not exactly a wonderful life even for those who get satisfaction from achieving everything on their list. That satisfaction is short-lived because the problem is that the list never dies. It just keeps coming back like a bad case of acne.

As it turns out, however, whatever your experiences might be, (and the examples above might not be yours) your life is unfolding perfectly.

Take a breath. Read that again. Your life experience, to date, is unfolding with **unforgiving perfection**.

That's a lot to wrap your head around, so let's start with a general explanation of what I mean, and we'll leave our specific exploration of the word 'unforgiving' until a little later.

Your 'perfect life' encompasses all the good things *and* the bad things you experience. Everyone loves the good things and tries to avoid the bad things...but they're valuable too!

Bad is good. You need to experience things you *don't like* so that you can figure out that you want something better! And pain helps inspire us to take action. In this sense, wherever you are in life and whatever you are experiencing, you're at the perfect place.

Let me give you some examples.

- 'I hate working at a pointless, dead-end job' gives birth to the thought 'I want to work at something fulfilling'. Maybe, just maybe, you even have a few ideas about what that fulfilling work might be.

- 'I hate living hand to mouth' gives birth to the powerful desire 'I want to be rich!' And maybe you figure out a few things you'd like to buy.

- 'I can't stand my partner, I never want to date trash like this again' gives birth to 'I want to date the perfect man/woman'. And maybe you get a few ideas about how that person might look and behave.

- 'I hate being tired all the time' gives birth to 'I want to feel bright, awake and vital'. And you might get a few ideas on how that's going to feel.

- 'I hate feeling sick' brings 'I want to feel healthy', and so on.

Your life, in this sense, can be seen as the unfolding journey of contrast between what you experience and what you want. It is only through experiencing the lack that you can find the strong passion, the unyielding drive and determination to manifest your dreams.

The Birth of Desire

Let's take a look at how your desires play out in real life.

Let's imagine that you're a young boy. One morning you're walking to school when a little dark-haired girl rides past you on a brand new bright red bike. Straight away you think, 'Oooh, yes, I'd love to have a red bike just like that one!'

Not having a red bike gives birth to your desire to own one. Then, based on that desire, a whole chain of events starts to unfold. First, since you're a child, the "I want" loop tape plays over and over in your head all day. It repeats when you go to sleep that night, and it repeats the next day, and the next night, and into the next week. And as long as the thought is in your head, you're doing what kids do; you're bugging your parents.

'Mom, can I have a bike? Mom, can I have a bike?' Even if you get a definitive no, you don't give up. You ask Dad. Then you go back to pestering Mom. After all, it's only a matter of time until one of them breaks, right?

It doesn't matter if you annoy them; it doesn't matter if they say 'No.' As far as you're concerned, the bike is on its way. It's not a question of 'if,' it's a matter of when. Your thoughts and words are completely unambiguous and consistent with your focused desire, no matter what is happening in the real world in front of you. One way or another you know that you're going to get that bike. For you, there are **no other options.**

Then, when you go to school the next day, you talk about the bike with your friends. 'I'm going to get a bike,' you say. 'It's going to be red, with gears and a basket up front. There are going to be pink flowers on it'

'Pink flowers?' says your friend 'That sounds a bit … girlie.'

So you refine your desire. 'Oh yeah, you're right. No flowers. Instead it's going to have red and orange flames painted down the side.' You effortlessly tweak your vision of perfection, never taking your eye off the prize for even a second.

Eventually, after you've been bugging your parents for a while, they start to change their tune. That kind of repetition will break *anyone* after a while! 'OK, you *might* be able to get a bike,' says your father during your after-dinner nagging session, 'but you have to earn it. You should get an after school job. When I was your age, I had a paper route.'

And so a new idea springs into your life. Great! This suits you fine. You'll happily do anything to get the bike...short of cleaning up your room. (You're only human, right?)

With the words 'earn it,' now etched into your brain, you look around and hey presto! There's a 'Delivery Boy Wanted' ad posted at the deli near your house. You inquire and you're hired! "When can you start?" Effortlessly you get the job, starting your route that very afternoon after school. The delivery boy job is an inspired action.

Slowly you save up your wages. You've done some online research and you know you need $100 to get the bike you desire, outfitted the way you want it. At $5.00 each week, that's 20 weeks which is around five months. All of a sudden you're a genius at math! (Mom and Dad should both like that.)

In 'kid years,' five months is a lifetime. So the idea comes to you that two jobs are surely better than one. You decide you can double-dip and work a second job at the local Dairy Queen after school. Surprise! That job also comes easily. So your bank balance starts to take off. It's amazing how things start to happen when you're consistently focused on your desire, thinking about it, talking about it and taking inspired actions.

After two weeks at your two jobs, you have $20.00. The next moment you have $40.00; only $60.00 to go. Almost before you can believe it — in just eight weeks, barely 2 months, not five -- you've got $80.00 in your stash.

Two weeks later you're showing your dad how far you've come when BAM! Another surprise comes your way. You father offers to match you, dollar for dollar. Awesome! It's as if some unseen force is conspiring with your desire to bring it to you more quickly and more amazingly that you had imagined in the first place.

That same day, with your father matching funds, you have $100.00 in your hands...and then some. And, as soon as the shop opens, it's a red letter day...or maybe Red Bike Day would be more accurate. Hurray!

So there you are, riding your brand new red bike through your neighborhood. You're strutting along the street (if you can strut on a bike), you're riding it reeeaal nice. All of a sudden who do you see? You see that very same girl go by. Only now she's riding next to a boy and they're holding hands while they ride. They look dreamily into each other's eyes, all of ten years old.

And what happens next? You get to school, your red bike almost forgotten.

'I want a girlfriend,' you confide to your best friend at break. 'And she's got to have a red bike too.'

Sound familiar?

OK, let's go back and replay this story with the Law of Attraction 'track' added.

The first thing you did was to **experience desire, expressed in a crystal clear thought:** 'I want a red bike'. You focused on the bike, learned everything about it, how much it cost, what all the trimmings were and so on. From the first moment, you had a clear expectation, an **unassailable faith** that you were going to own that bike *even though you didn't have any idea of how.*

You didn't, as adults tend to do, entertain doubts. You didn't start an internal dialogue saying things like 'I don't really deserve this bike,' or 'This bike is too good for me,' or 'I'll never be able to afford this bike.' These are contradictory thoughts which can cause the Law of Attraction to manifest ambiguous results, and the lack of them is why children seem to get so much of what they want in their young lives.

Everything that you achieve working with the Law of Attraction starts with a clear, unambiguous thought. You focus on that thought consistently, during every waking moment as only children can do. It's powerful.

After you 'thought' about the red bike, you took it to the next level of manifesting. The next thing you did was **utilize the power of words.** In speaking to your friends, family and anyone else you could find, you added even more power to your 'summoning' (another word for attracting.) With words, you 'polarize' the experience, event or possession that you're after so it's attracted to you like a magnet. Also, when you talk to people about your desires, you're giving them the chance to add their own suggestions, contributions and connections.

In this case, words to classmates led to a refinement of your desire for how the bike would be accessorized. Words also prompted the boy's father to suggest getting a job. What a great idea! What an inspiration!

With desire and words working for you, your next step was to take action. But you didn't run around taking random action. That can be counterproductive. Instead, the third thing you did was perhaps the hardest thing of all. You did nothing, but **wait to be stimulated to take inspired action**. You waited for that 'Aha!' moment when an idea, suggestion or connection suddenly presents itself to you and it just feels 'right.'

In this case, the 'right' idea was a delivery job which, in turn, brought the notion of a second job, accelerating the whole process.

Then, just when you thought you knew exactly what was coming something even better turns up! In this case, the last minute doubling of the cash so that you ended up with more than $100 and that became the bike and 'all the trimmings.'

And remember the end of this particularly human story. The moment we humans manifest our desires, we immediately focus on the next desire.

Desire in Real Life

You now know how manifesting with the Law of Attraction works in everyday life. So how can you make it work for YOU?

When you follow the concept of desire through to its logical conclusion, you'll notice an amazing end result. The physical world operates according to the Law of Attraction -- meaning in practice that what you think about, talk about and act upon you attract to yourself -- *so your ability to manifest your desires is limitless.*

In fact, everything in your life was brought there by means of the Law of Attraction. Therefore, working backwards, everything in your life got there by **the formative means of your own thoughts.**

Yes, you create your own world. You create *everyone in* it. You create *everything* it. The entire physical reality of your life is your own creation and, therefore (and here's the part that so many people don't like) **it is your own responsibility.**

It's time to give up pointing fingers. Gone are the days of blaming anyone or anything other than your own good self for your situation. There's no point in crying out 'Why do bad things happen to me?!' The honest truth is that nothing happens *to* you. You make it all happen, starting with the thoughts in your head.

Did you bring all the friendships, the fantastic health, the financial wealth, the awesome home, the great job, the beautiful wife, the handsome husband, the toe-curling sex -- all that good stuff to your life? Yes, you did. (Well done!)

But does this mean you brought the bad as well as the good? Did you bring the loneliness, the obesity, the poverty, the sickness, the accidents -- all that terrible stuff? The answer, thought it may be hard to hear, is "Yes." It's all you. And it's all by means of the Law of Attraction...and therefore, in turn, by your own focused thought, intended words and inspired actions.

Let me give you an example from my life.

Around about two years ago, Angela and I were living in Sydney on the Northern Beaches in a rented house. We were both eager to buy our own home. We'd had enough of nosy landlords, of rent increases and circumstances beyond our control. We'd had enough of rentals and sublets that no one really cared about or took the time and money to maintain. We wanted our own house. We wanted to make our own improvements and our own decisions. In short we wanted to 'be the boss' of us. Also we knew it made the most long term financial sense.

More than anything, I had a vision of sledge-hammering my way through some dry-wall, just bashing it down wildly as I made modifications to my own house. Man, was that going to feel GREAT!

Having a house became a MUST HAVE. We had the will and we sure as shooting planned on finding a way.

So then we did what lots of people do. We shifted our focus from the 'What If' and got caught up in the 'What Is'. In other words, we focused on reality, what existed in front of us at that moment. We started a house hunting campaign. Like generals, we purchased newspapers, magazines and buying guides. We dedicated our weekends to meeting with realtors and visiting potential properties. We subscribed to realtor web sites, received and read daily emailed reports.

Our problem was that everything was crazy expensive in Sydney, as it is metropolitan areas around the world. We wanted to live in Sydney in our own house, but when it came down to the financial reality in front of us, we just couldn't afford to.

Did we let that get us down? No way, baby.

Still focusing on the 'What Is', we started to look outside of Sydney.

As we moved further from the heart of Sydney, we found cheaper places. Unfortunately we just couldn't see how we could make these remote locations work with our lifestyle, especially with the work we both do. For me, access to an international airport is imperative. For my wife, access to her friends and business contacts is imperative. Finally, the kids are about to go to school and we had grown attached to the schools where we were already living.

In the end, after a harsh dose of 'What Is,' we gave up. Looking back, I'm surprised that we didn't recognize earlier that we were going *against the flow*. We could see what we wanted, but not *how* to make it happen. Anyway, we finally flopped down in a crying heap and gave up. That turned out to be a **genius move!**

Instead of struggling with the 'What Is,' we finally started to focus on *what we wanted*. 'What if there was a place that fit all our specifications and we could afford it and it was in the area we wanted?' Can you see where this is going? We started talking about what we *wanted*. We started playing games around what we wanted.

We got some notebooks and put them in the car, by the bed and on the kitchen table. And then we started to put our prefect house, our wildest dream home and all of its desirable features, into words and onto paper. We didn't worry about what we thought was possible; we left our analytical, left brains out of it and listened to our irrepressible inner children instead. We let our 'right brains' run free!

We were very clear that this wasn't about reality. We'd done that, and 'What Is' had failed us. Now it was time to focus on the 'What If' fantasy. The house we *would* have if we *could* have the house we wanted.

We listed things like a fireplace, an open kitchen, and 3 bedrooms, no–4 bedrooms! Yeah, that's the stuff. We wanted floorboards in open areas, carpet in the bedrooms. We wanted lovely neighbours whom we couldn't see easily from our windows or in the back yard on all sides. We wanted a flat back yard for our kids and the dog, when he or she came along. We wanted, we wanted, we wanted.

Then we started to **put those thoughts into word form.**

We spoke to people about our dreams and desires. We called a home loan specialist and had him run the numbers. We spoke to friends, to family, and to anyone who would listen at parties about the home we were hoping to have.

And then, when we were done, we just let it go. We should've probably had a ceremony where we burned the lists, offering them up to a higher power.

As it was, I think we just ran the idea into the ground, ran out of new things to say and, simply put, ran out of juice, stopped talking and thinking and soon forgot about it. We didn't have the power to manifest our dream house from 'What Is' and it looked as though we weren't going to get it with 'What If' either.

We were wrong. A higher power came along, and not by accident. Our thoughts had attracted like thoughts, like circumstances, like conversations and aligned connections. The Law of Attraction had been working the whole time. Now, based on our clear expressions of desire, even though *we* weren't working on the Law of Attraction, it was working *for us*.

Of course, it didn't show up in any way we might've expected. It didn't even show up in a way anyone would want it to, my wife and I least of all.

My grandmother on my mother's side mother died very unexpectedly. She was quite the rebel and quite the adventurer, my grandmother, traveling the world and wringing the most out of life. A few days before she died, in her eighties, she was talking excitedly about a trip to Hawaii!

We were shocked and saddened when it happened and we still miss her very much today.

We were surprised to learn that she had left us quite a large inheritance. And we were even more surprised when my parents decided to lend a hand to our house-hunting efforts with a significant financial gift of their own. It was like magic! All of a sudden we had a deposit. It was the very thing we'd been unable to manage on our own. Thank you Grandma! And you, too, Mom and Dad.

It was stunning. In the course of a single day...a single hour...a single moment, really, things went from impossible to possible. Or, put another way, we went from 'we couldn't imagine how it would happen' to 'we could see clearly how it was going to happen'. Once we stopped being hung up trying to figure out every detail of *how* it was going to happen, we cleared the way for it to come together in its own way. And better than we could've imagined!

As long as we had tried to force it, the entire desire was blocked. It was **getting out of our own way** that did it.

Immediately after this deposit manifested itself, another cute little thing happened. I got a call from our landlord asking if he could drop by. He sounded a little weird, by which I mean to say, stranger than usual. I met him at the door the next morning.

'I think I have some bad news,' he said with a faint smile on his face and a note in his hand. He appeared to actually *enjoy* delivering the bad news to us.

'Yeah, I don't think so,' I said. I was confident. He was a bit surprised.

'No, really I do,' he said. 'It's really bad news, you're going to hate it.' Was he smiling even more? 'You have thirty days to vacate the premises. Your twelve month lease has expired and we've decided we want to move into the house ourselves.'

'And how is that bad news?' I said. You see, I already saw this as a positive step towards getting our new house—another little sign saying IT'S TIME TO DO THIS NOW!

Sure enough, my wife checked her email that day and BAM. There it was. The house we were going to buy. It was cute and sweet with a fireplace and floorboards and carpets and level block and backyard and on and on. So I got the call that she'd found a house that she loves and will I come see it?

I surprised her (and me, too) with what I told her. "Buy it," I said, without even seeing a photo. "Put an offer on it NOW...today...this morning. If it's that clear to you" (and from the sound in her voice, I knew it was), "Then do it."

So she did. From memory I wasn't even in the city. We spoke by phone to the realtor, and it turned out the house was to be auctioned in a month or so. Rather than wait for the auction, however, we put on an offer on it that day, only to find 24 hours later that our offer was not acceptable to the owner. So now we went back to the agent and asked her help. She was very nice, very supportive. What should we do? 'Make the biggest offer you can possibly afford,' she said.

We made a second offer that maxed us out; it was the very most we could pay under the circumstances. The buyer accepted our offer that day, even though he was in Singapore at the time. The house never went to auction...because we bought it.

We bought the house and moved in just before we were kicked out of our last rental house ever… and we live in our dream house today. And you know what? It's even better than we were able to imagine. We're in a perfectly quiet neighborhood that is also within five minutes' walk of a beautiful lake, and ten minutes' walk from the ocean. We even have some shops about 5 minutes' walk away for little conveniences, plus my wife's favorite Chinese restaurant and the best fish and chips shop in town are just around the corner. And these are things we hadn't even put on our list!

Here's an interesting footnote to this part of the story. We found out after the event that other, larger offers had come in later when the house was in escrow, but the owner had refused these on the basis that we'd done everything right, with honesty and integrity.

A Law That's Implacable… Like Gravity

When you first hear about the Law of Attraction you think, 'I just have to 'want' something to get it? It couldn't be that easy.' After all, you've been wanting a couple of million dollars in the bank for years…not to mention a sweet place to live, a flashy sports car, a hot girlfriend, cool friends and a villa in France.

So what gives, Law of Attraction, if all it takes is 'want,' then why don't I have everything I want *right now*?

Your instinct about 'too easy' is right. It turns out that utilizing the power of the Law of Attraction is a little trickier than it first seems. Not that the Law of Attraction is hard; you just need to understand how to work with it.

Here's what I needed to understand to realize that the Law of Attraction does, indeed, work in real life.

The Law of Attraction is an 'equal opportunity' force, like gravity. Gravity doesn't discriminate. Gravity doesn't say 'Hey, I love this apple! I'm going to work for this apple. I don't like oranges, or any of the other apples, so they can all just float off into space without me.' Gravity applies equally to everything every time, implacably, without judgment. It doesn't pick and choose.

The Law of Attraction is the same.

You say, 'I want to feel great,' and the Law of Attraction delivers great to your doorstep. You say, 'I want to feel terrible', and the same principle will bring you a whole lot of pain and suffering.

With the Law of Attraction, you get back what you put out.

If you say, 'I want a million dollars,' the Law of Attraction works to bring a million dollars to you. However if you qualify that statement and say, 'I want a million dollars *but I'll never get a million dollars*,' then you're giving the Law of Attraction conflicting instructions. Who knows what it will bring you, if anything, since contradictory forces cancel each other out.

I've also been better able to 'get' the Law of Attraction since I realized that it rarely delivers me the object of my desire neatly packaged in a FedEx box addressed to Tim Levy, delivered to my door by an enthusiastic man in shorts and white knee-high socks. It works a little more indirectly, although just as powerfully.

In addition to tangible things, I've learned that The Law of Attraction delivers something that helps bring tangible things to me:

- **New impulses, ideas and thoughts**
- **Connections with new people**, places and businesses
- **Motivations**, guiding feelings and emotions

- **What people tend to refer to as 'coincidences'**, although some would argue there is no such thing, merely events orchestrated by the Law of Attraction

- **What people call 'omens'**; signs that mean something to you one way or another; signs that bring you to new thoughts, words and actions

It is in these more subtle ways that the Law of Attraction operates. At first, what's happening may seem unrelated to your desires. In time, as you learn to pay more and more attention and become fluent in the 'language' of the Law, it becomes louder, clearer and less ambiguous... until finally, it's unmistakable.

Are you getting the picture? The Law of Attraction doesn't work with the U.S. Postal Service to 'deliver the goods.' It works with **inspiration, connection and specific events**. So keep an eye out for these kinds of things in your day-to-day life.

With that point made, it's time to get back to how it works; the implacable, non-judgmental nature of the Law of Attraction.

Let's say that you're wandering along through life, everything is fine, everything is good when suddenly a memo turns up saying the boss wants to see you. Immediately a part of your mind freaks out and says, 'He's going to fire me. I know it. Something bad is going to happen, I know it!' It's hard to make that thought go away, isn't it?

It's hard, but not impossible. You'll need to learn some discipline so that you can tame these kinds of thoughts -- the unhelpful, self-negating internal monologue we refer to as **Brain Chatter** -- since the Law of Attraction will immediately start to bring this to you. (Don't worry about Brain Chatter right now. We'll talk about it in greater detail later in the book)

In response to your mental meltdown, the Law of Attraction might start by bringing you some similar thoughts, like, 'He fired my buddy Bob just like this. It all started with a memo' or, 'Bad things always happen to me on Fridays'.

Or the Law of Attraction might bring you some similar words. Let's say you lean over to the next desk and say to your co-worker Susie, 'Hey Susie, did you get a memo like this?'

'No, what's in it?' asks Susie.

'The boss wants to see me. Sounds weird, right?' you say.

'Wow. That's how Bob got fired, remember?'

This is Law of Attraction in action. It brings the thoughts, words and connections that are **aligned with your desire** right to your door. It's implacable like gravity so it gives equal weight to what you want (in the positive way) and what you don't want (in a negative way).

Bring Me a Bunny
This is an important point. I've already made it before but, since **repetition is the mother of learning**, I'll say it again. The Law of Attraction doesn't know the difference between 'I want a bunny,' and 'I don't want a bunny.' It doesn't 'rank' one above the other. All the Law of Attraction does is bring you what you think about whether you're phrasing it positively or negatively. It doesn't really hear 'I want' or 'I don't want'. It just hears 'bunny'.

This means that you need to take **personal responsibility** to **always ask for what you want clearly and without conflict**. And of course, you want to ask for what you want rather than what you don't want. This means you'll be looking for positive statements rather than a negative one. These are tough skills to master, since most people are not naturally disciplined about such things. That's okay. It comes more naturally with practice.

Here's an example from the Levy House. We don't watch television news and we don't read newspapers. We're aware that those media report on sensational stories because they attract viewers and Nielsen ratings and advertising dollars. As a result, the news is rife with murder, death and mayhem. If there's a new exhibit at the art gallery, they won't cover it. If there's a painting stolen or a murder right there on the gallery floor, then the exhibit is the news...as the scene set for "Grisly Murder at New Art Exhibit." The more graphic and embarrassing the murder, war or Hollywood scandal is, the better.

No one at my house wants to or needs to focus on these things. So as part of a process of removing the thoughts we don't want, leaving only the thoughts that we do, we've disciplined ourselves to avoid that kind of news coverage.

Clarifying Your Thoughts

It's time to use your imagination again. Let's imagine for a moment that you have a series of thoughts during the course of a day and that you write them down for later analysis. We'll list them out here.

- I hate my job
- I hate my boss
- I can't stand my little grey cubicle
- I want to leave right now and never come back
- I don't mind getting paid, though
- I love getting a regular check every month
- I love all the stuff I can buy with that check
- I don't mind *all* of my co-workers
- I think my red socks are nifty

Okay. That's just a selection of random thoughts. You can imagine the dozens more that go with them. Now comes the important task:

Can you look at those thoughts and pick out the ones that are going to help you, with regard to the Law of Attraction? It's these two:

- I love getting a regular check every month
- I love all the stuff I can buy with that check

Why do these thoughts 'rate' with regard to the Law of Attraction? These thoughts are **positive statements about what you actually desire,** rather than negative statements about what you don't want. As such they're going to bring you what you desire, rather than what you don't.

The process we refer to as organizing or disciplining your thoughts means, simply, letting go of or re-phrasing every thought except those (like the two we picked out) that help you attract what you desire. Release the others from your mind, forever. You don't need to use them, so lose them. **Simply choose not to think those thoughts.**

Sometimes useless, defeating thoughts rush in before you have a chance to stop them. When that happens, you can choose to **replace them with better thoughts** that reflect your desires as opposed to your fears, doubts or conflicts. Here is a set of detailed, unambiguous thoughts to replace the unfocused thoughts above:

I want a job where I get to be outside all the time and I earn a large bunch of money

- I want a boss who is just great, someone I could see as a friend, someone whose values I agree with and treats me right, someone who looks out for me as well as his/her own agenda, someone I can trust

- I want to work outside in the wild where I get to walk in the forest and take a canoe across the lake every day
- I can't wait to find my new job and to do it every day
- I want to get paid generously, reflecting the value of my work fairly. I also want to get recognition, awards and bonuses at the end of every year
- I love getting a regular check every month *(unchanged)*
- I love all the stuff I can buy with that check *(unchanged)*
- I want to work with people I really like and who like me
- I think my red socks are nifty and I want to have so much money that I can buy new pairs whenever I like

What we now have is a set of non-conflicting and therefore unambiguous desires that are stated clearly. What's interesting is that in clarifying your desires you are likely to trigger a mental chain-reaction. You might think of some more details about what you desire. You might have some ideas about what you could do to get closer to those desires in a fun way. You might think of someone you could call or an email you might send.

At any rate, the process of becoming conscious of your thoughts and then self-editing them to reflect your desires without conflict is what we refer to as **organizing your thoughts and disciplining your mind.**

It's quite a tricky process at first when you're not used to it. Most people produce a bonanza of conflicted, fearful, doubtful or just plain negative thoughts. We talk about that in the next chapter.

What you might want to do, for now, is take the time to **write out these thoughts** like we just did above, and then **assess them** with regard to the Law of Attraction. Are your thoughts serving you by bringing things you want, or not? If not, you need to get rid of the problem thoughts and, if possible, convert them into thoughts that are positive statements of your desires as in the example above.

The good news is that it gets easier and easier until it becomes a habit. And then, you don't even notice you're doing it. There's no effort involved – you just **watch your desires unfold before you**. Fun!

Brain Chatter and Ego

This section is a little different from the others in this book. It's from an article that appeared in 'Urban Enlightenment' the monthly column I write for Australia's favorite holistic magazine; Living Now.

It is also sent free to everyone who has joined my newsletters at www.thelifesummit.com. *I think it fits perfectly into our discussion.*

I wish I was perfectly enlightened, perfectly aligned, perfectly clear. Instead, I'm normal. By that, I mean my brain is a bit of a mess most of the time. And it turns out that there's a reason...apart from the obvious conclusion that I'm only human.

The problem is that I carry around inside my head not one, but several voices. There's the one I like and then there's the other one that...well... let's just say that it's the little mongrel that drives me mental!

The voice I like speaks to me from the calm, collected, centered part of me that makes rational, considered, solid decisions. This part of me has the capacity for **perspective beyond the moment**. It can speak of joy and sadness and everything in between. It likes to keep the perspective that I'm **a spiritual being having a human experience** rather than the other way around. This is the bit that I like to think of as *who I really am.*

But there's another clamoring for my attention...an annoying voice that I could easily do without. *This* voice is loud, convincing and comes from the part of me that lives stressfully, moment to moment. This voice is, for the most part, a trouble-maker. Unfortunately, it's also a terrific impersonator. My 'negative self' spends a lot of time pretending to be the other, more thoughtful me – and gets away with it more often than I care to admit!

This other voice is smart as a whip and knows just how to press my buttons. And it's quick...in the blink of an eye it can manufacture all kinds of snide comments and little jabs. My negative voice is fast as a panther in making his judgments, fears and concerns known loudly and clearly. And did I mention dramatic?

'We'll never get rich, we're going to be poor forever!' the voice laments as you open a phone bill, never stopping to consider that you can pay the bill comfortably and always have up until now.

'This is going to be cancer, I can feel it!' the voice says as you sit waiting in the doctor's office for a report. 'After all, one in eight people die of Cancer plus we used to smoke!' says the voice, not taking into account that you've been just fine up until now.

This is the same voice that in the previous chapter was fretting, 'We're going to be fired and then we're going to be broke! We're going to lose the house and live on the street!' In response to the unexpected email from the boss. This voice doesn't consider that you've held this job successfully for several years. This part of you doesn't remember that the boss generally only emails you to take you to lunch. It just yells 'Panic stations, everyone, and right NOW!'

This voice is pretty compelling, right? And it's so quick, so automatic and reflexive that **it's easy to mistake it for the truth.** And yet, most of the time, it's not.

Sure – this hyper-vigilant part of you is looking out for your best interests, like a sailor watching for rocks from the crow's nest of your mind. It has **the first answer.** It sometimes has **the louder answer.** It almost always has a **stressful, fearful answer** that would have you live in those emotion states perpetually. But...here's the 'big idea': that this part of you doesn't always, or even often, have **the best answer.**

Yet you listen to it. We all do. And this part of you contributes massively towards the kind of ambiguity that will derail your efforts regarding the Law of Attraction.

I call this voice my 'Brain Chatter.' It feels very **ego-driven** to me, and not the kind of advice I'd want to use to run my life. I'd much prefer to listen to that more considered, fun-loving, authentic part of me that can be heard when the brain chatter is not active. Actually, given a choice, I'd prefer to listen to the soul or spirit part of me that predates even that consciousness...although to be honest, I don't have that part of me on speed dial.

To make a long story short — or is it too late for that? -- I'm learning, day by day, to identify brain chatter for what it is. It's not truth, not reality, not even good advice! It's part gossip, part drama and part hot air from a part of you that delights in that kind of thing *for its own sake.* It's chatter!

I'm getting good at recognizing when it's brain chatter talking as opposed to the more profound, conscious me. And when I *do* recognize a thought that comes from this chatter place, I 'channel' The Beatles. I 'let it be.'

Thoughts are like people, and they all deserve a little respect. So acknowledge your Brain Chatter thoughts when they occur. Give them a nod, a smile, and a wave as they pass through your consciousness. Brain Chatter isn't *trying* to foul you up. It's actually looking out for your best interests. Be glad it's there.

'We're going to have to get rid of the dog or we'll slip on one of these yellow puddles, break our leg, lose our job and ultimately die!' it tells me as we step around another pool of stinky carpet dampness. 'This is a PANIC SITUATION!' it yells.

I love it – what a great voice!

So I just nod, smile and wave, deliberately forgetting that it ever even spoke. I think of it as comic relief as opposed to reality and remember that it's not the part of me that should control my decision-making.

Find Clarity in Meditation

Did you enjoy the article in the last chapter? I hope so. As you now know, the Law of Attraction brings you anything you focus on in a non-judgmental, implacable way. What you need to do, therefore, is **to think about, communicate and act** on your desires in only a positive, unambiguous and consistent way.

You need to become conscious of your thoughts and learn to control them until you have only those that support your desires. Although this comes easily with practice, it can be tricky at first. With that in mind, I recommend that you **meditate.**

When I am in a meditative state, free of all other distractions, I find that I make the best progress in organizing my thoughts. It is in meditation that I am most aware of my thoughts. It makes logical sense, therefore, that it is in meditation that I have the best chance of deciding which thoughts are aligned with my desires and which thoughts are not. Then, having become more aware of them, I simply keep the ones I want and release the ones I don't want. On the odd occasion I re-phrase my negative thoughts into positive ones. Then, just for good measure, I release those too.

If you've been at all active in the self-help, self-improvement, spiritual or religious genres, chances are you've heard all about meditation. While an in-depth discussion of meditation is beyond the scope of this book, I thought it might be good to include a rough and ready **layman's guide** to this practice before moving onto a meditation created specifically for use with the Law of Attraction.

So here is my one-paragraph definition of meditation.

> *Meditation is when you quiet your mind until you have no thoughts left at all. Meditation is simply the absence of all thoughts. Meditation is that quiet place you find in the gap between your thoughts.*

Let's do the math here. If you aren't thinking about anything, then it logically follows that you cannot be entertaining conflicting thoughts either, right? So a meditative state where your mind is clear is a powerful and unambiguous state in which to work with the Law of Attraction.

Rough and ready guide...finished! I promised you it would be quick. And if you wish to know more about meditation, you can find material in every bookshop, church and place of worship; or of course, you can Google it.

Given that you need to organize your thoughts towards a consistent, unambiguous and focused desire, it's clear that meditation is an obviously useful technique. But what kind of meditation? To answer that, here's a quick personal note on heavy, technical meditation. The kind you do in a room full of incense with people trying to 'vibrate' to a higher consciousness.

I find that this kind of all-or-nothing meditation, in the Transcendental Meditation form, a little hard to maintain. I'm not the kind of guy to retreat to a cave in the Himalayas for ten years trying to figure out how many angels can fit on the head of a pin.

My life is an active one with active desires. Quite often I'm *doing* something. I am results-oriented more than process-oriented, so I've created for myself a simple, everyday meditation practice that is aimed at bringing daily results.

5 Things You Can Do For A Results-Oriented Meditation

☐ <u>Chose the Right Location</u> – It's said that the three most important words in real estate are 'location, location, location.' This is also true in meditation. So I start by selecting somewhere nice to sit. I like nature and I happen to live near a lake. So I go and find a quiet spot near the edge of the lake. Meditating in front of the TV, on a train, or while the kids are pestering you about dinner is possible, and I've done it. It's just not as good as meditating in a quiet spot.

For me, a simple, quiet spot is nowhere near as good as a quiet lake with a vista of rolling green hills behind it. That I care about the view is ironic considering what comes next:

☐ <u>Close your Eyes and Focus on your Breath</u> - When you meditate, you close your eyes...so I don't even see the lake *or* the rolling hills! Absurd, isn't it? Still, I find that simply being there makes all the difference. With my eyes closed, I start to focus on my breathing which, quite naturally, starts to slow down.

They say that the yogis actually stop breathing altogether...although I don't recommend going that far.

☐ Quiet Your Thoughts - Next, I start to quiet my thoughts by simply letting them go. If a thought jumps into my head at this time like, 'My goodness I left the iron on!' then I simply let the thought fly out the way it came in. Or I create a visual picture. I imagine the thought written on a page that flies out of my mind's eye and blows away like dandelion seeds in the wind.

I do this for as long as it takes to get to a place of total calm, where I can just 'be' at least a moment or two without any thoughts...just me, sitting by the lake with space in my head. This typically takes around **five or ten minutes**, but of course, sometimes it doesn't happen at all. That's okay. You're not trying to be perfect.

The nice thing about meditation is that it simply doesn't matter. You just let that go too and keep going!

☐ Focus On Your Desire - Now I start to focus on what I want. It's in meditation that I can do this without any ambiguity, without any mental clashes that might bring conflicted results from the Law of Attraction. It's easy; I just think about what I want in words, in pictures, in actions, or whatever.

I try to keep this fairly consistent from day to day because I know my desires are coming closer and closer to manifesting as I repeat them in my mind's eye.

☐ Live Your Desire As If It Were Here NOW - This step in my meditation is where the real work...and the real progress is. I now start to **experience those desires in my mind in the present tense.** In this sacred place I'm working directly with the Law of Attraction, so I **let go any reservations** I might have. This is tricky for some because they're so hung up on 'what is'.

In other words, some people want to know, 'How can I experience my desire in the present when my desire *isn't actually here* right now?' There's an expression – Fake it until you make it. That's what you do. *Pretend* that it's real right now. Honestly, don't worry too much. Just enjoy it!

For example, I might imagine money in my bank account. I see myself picking up the checks from my mail box, transferring e-cash with PayPal. I see myself folding the bills into my wallet, then spending the money on a great romantic dinner at a restaurant that my wife and I adore, laughing with her as we clink our glasses.

I see myself smiling as I play with my kids, content in the knowledge that their health and education needs are paid for...swelling with energy to do more and more. It's a kick. What's not to love?

And that's it. Simple. Fun. Done. And for me, the cornerstone to my daily work manifesting the life of my dreams. Although there is an **extra step** that sometimes happens. If it doesn't what do I do? Of course, I simply smile and let that go too.

Something You Don't Have to Do

There are many ways I can be proactive in my meditation. But one thing doesn't require any effort on my part at all. It happens on its own...or doesn't happen at all. If it does; that's great. And if it doesn't, don't sweat it since you can't make it happen by force.

So I'm in my meditation state. I focus on my desires and then charge them up with the positive emotions that are generated from 'living' those desires as I visualize them happening in the 'now'.

Here's what happens for me next, and this is key. It's in this highly charged, positive, unambiguous and feel-good place that the Law of Attraction starts to work.

I find that as I'm imagining these things I want, other thoughts start to simply pop into my head. Maybe I remember someone I haven't thought of in a while, and I imagine myself calling them. Maybe I think about how cool it would be to start up a new business. Maybe I imagine giving my wife an unanticipated bunch of flowers and the amazing things that might just follow.

I perceive these great-feeling ideas coming from a place of unambiguously expressed desires and *inspired ideas, thoughts and actions*. These are my **inspired actions**. They come from my most uplifted spirit and my clearest mind. These are the thoughts I jot down later if I can, making definitive plans to act on them even if they don't make much sense to me at the time. These are frequently the 'Eureka!' moments that drive my life in unanticipated and wonderful directions.

Inspiration is elusive. It doesn't always happen, but when it does, attention must be paid. I don't know where those thoughts, words and inspired actions come from, but I do know that they're always amazing. Even if it's just a deeper, unconscious part of me talking, that part of me clearly knows something I don't, because the ideas that come into my head are quite often very right-brained and creative.

They are often almost outlandish, too. That's part of the fun. One way or another, these thoughts always bring fantastic variety, excitement and wealth into my life. Who am I to complain?!

I often embark on a meditation 'campaign' where my goal is to meditate every day, or maybe every day for a month or every day for 90 days. That kind of thing appeals to my more competitive nature. And you know what happens if I don't actually do my meditation on the schedule I've laid out for myself? I relax…smile…and let that go, too.

Detachment

Okay, if you've been reading the Life Summit from the beginning, here's what you now have in your possession:

- **A basic understanding** of the Law of Attraction, including what is it and how it works
- **An emerging focus** on clear, unambiguous and consistently expressed desires
- **An understanding of the power of thoughts**, words and inspired actions
- **An understanding of the importance of organizing** your thoughts, perhaps with the assistance of a daily meditation

Now we come to a discussion of the next critical concept in the Law of Attraction. This is called *detachment*. You've probably heard the enlightened gurus suggesting that if you can master the art of detachment, that you'll live a long and happy life. A life lived detached is a life lived without stress.

If only it were that simple! The plain truth is that detachment is definitely tricky and probably impossible. At least it feels impossible most of the time.

This is especially true of today's instant gratification culture where we are taught that we can have what we want now. Need coffee? Instant coffee. Need food? Fast food...with drive-through convenience, no less. Need a haircut? Walk-in salons. We've grown accustomed to the world interpreting our desires as *demands of the utmost importance and urgency.*

So how does detachment, also known as 'giving up desire,' fit into that? At first glance, it just plain doesn't.

Of course we're attached to our desires! After all, they're our desires, right? Of course we're attached to every minute detail of our lives. After all they're our very lives we're talking about, right? Why would we willingly give up any desire?

Actually, I saw a terrific example of this just yesterday. I was at the mall with my children during a weekday of the school holidays. You'll all relate to this I'm sure.

The mall is always full. The parents of younger children like myself are frequently lured there with the promise of free half-hour live shows themed on cartoons like 'Bob the Builder' and 'Hannah Montana.' It's a delightful place. Someone else has the job of distracting my kids for a while.

So there we were with other parents and kids, waiting in line for the day's show. Actually it wasn't a show; it turned out to be a workshop entitled 'Designing Donuts' that the local Krispie Kreme shop was offering every 30 minutes from 10 a.m. until noon. Each child was given a donut and encouraged to decorate to their sugar-loving heart's content with as much frosting and as many sprinkles as they could. It wasn't exactly what I would call a 'healthy' kids outing, but let's set that aside for the moment.

Here's the important part. The next show was set for 11 a.m. And although the frosting was still in good supply, the sweet, friendly gang from Krispie Kreme had run out of sprinkles. It was understandable. One look at the gooey faces of the kids from the previous workshop told the whole story. They were *covered* in sprinkles! (And smiles, too.)

As the clock struck 11 a.m., a Krispie Kreme employee had taken off at a frantic run to get more sprinkles. The main Krispie Kreme store was just a few storefronts away, so the delay was going to be minimal...five or six minutes at the most.

Now, do you think the parents were patient and tolerant about this itty bitty delay which had been thoughtfully and apologetically explained by the remaining staff? Not a chance. They hissed and moaned, wriggled and fussed. Not the kids! I'm talking about the parents here. The children were fine. The parents who were accustomed to being served on demand looked furiously at their watches and bitched to each other than the entire thing was *several minutes late* and their time was being wasted and who was going to compensate them for the wait?

Now that is attachment. They were so attached to a free children's activity starting exactly on time that they started to get angry. And I mean truly angry, not just playing around. They complained, talked about going to management; the whole nine yards. It was staggering.

But let's be honest. We can all be a little like that, right? We get 'invested' in an outcome and become enraged when we don't get out way. And *that's* why it feels like you're living contrary to nature when someone asks you to be detached.

Defining Detachment

So what does detachment really mean? Good question! It's all about how you define the word. To illustrate my definition of detachment, let's start with a 'real life' story that comes from your imagination.

Let's say that you're rolling through life happy as pie, expecting to get a super seventeenth birthday present coming up at the end of the week. Since you're almost grown up, the present is actually a car. Yes, your first car. You've seen all the signs: the huddled conversations between the parents...the fact that your older sister got hers when she was turning 17. You've been dropping hints and everything is going according to plan.

You wake up birthday morning; your heart is beating so hard that you can barely breathe. You open the front door and there it is shiny and sleek and brand spanking new with a big red ribbon: a scooter.

Huh? What? This can't be. How are you going to cruise for hotties with that?! Suddenly **the gap between what you were expecting and what actually happened** opens up before you like a black chasm filled with ravenous crocodiles. The pain of this gap is so intense that you cannot speak.

Your parents interpret this lack of words as joy and boy, are they wrong. They're grinning from ear to ear like Halloween pumpkins. Your heart is breaking and your head is about to explode. This is a moment when a little detachment would be helpful.

In the Western world, detachment is defined as **unlinking yourself from your feelings and emotions**. According to that definition, instead of feeling the pain of heart-crushing disappointment, you opt to feel nothing. You become detached. This interpretation of detachment leads people to believe that they should detach themselves from their lives, thereby relieving themselves of the potential for pain by letting go of their desires before they even have them. By this interpretation

No desires = no disappointment = no pain

No joy either. So I definitely don't mean detachment like that.

In the Eastern world, however, detachment is defined differently. Detachment means **releasing the manner of the manifestation of your desires to a higher power.** Defined this way, detachment means that even though you received a scooter instead of the car of your dreams (or even a beat-up jalopy), your desire is coming to you perfectly, only in a different form than you had imagined.

Hello Desire, Good-bye 'How'

Detachment is releasing the 'How' of the manifestation of your desires.

And how will this happen? It's the understanding that *your* job is to define your desires with focused, clear, unambiguous and consistent thoughts ... nothing more, nothing less. The Law of Attraction will do the rest, bringing you the perfect answer according to its perspective -- which is simply a wider, better, more enlightened perspective than your own.

Why ask why? Just because you don't know all the facts in the here-and-now to understand why things are unfolding in the way that they are, that's no reason to become angry, feel disappointed, or get stressed out.

When the Universe (or God...or however you think of it) is answering your prayers, surely it has a broader perspective than your own! Or, put even more simply, **the Universe knows better** than you. So if the Universe is giving you a scooter then be happy with your scooter knowing that it's for your own highest good.

By accepting what has come into your experience as **the ideal implementation of your desires,** you pave the way for a joyous life watching events unfold in their own perfect, charming and usually unexpected way. Goodness knows I can almost never see what's coming and *that's where the fun is!*

Suddenly you're free! You're not detached from your desires, you're detached from the process of bringing them into reality. That's not your job. The Law of Attraction figures out 'how' your desires will manifest.

When you detach, you **release your conscious mind from trying to figure out beforehand exactly the way in which everything is going**

to unfold. Detachment means giving your brain clear instructions to release the 'how' from its possessive claws and let something else – in this case the Law of Attraction – do the work. Invariably, of course, our conscious minds have problems with this. The conscious mind is addicted to anticipation; it just LOVES imagining the future in minute detail. And it plays back its imagined vision of the future over and over again like a loop tape. Unfortunately, your conscious mind then takes the hardest hit when things don't turn out exactly according to your mental plan.

Detachment is the understanding that from your **limited personal perspective,** you simply don't know everything. You know enough to know that life is completely unpredictable, so **stop predicting**! Or at least, release your attachment to any specific prediction in favor of joyously observing life unfold perfectly without any help from you other than your clear, unambiguous, consistent thoughts about your desires.

This is one of the great amusing tricks of the Law of Attraction. It brings you what you desire, what you focus on unflinchingly and unambiguously, in the form of *its* choice. Not yours. Quite often the desire turns up as you thought it might; sometimes it doesn't. **Detachment allows you to be happy either way.**

The great good fun of life is watching these desires manifest in front of you in myriad, unimaginable forms, and trusting that those forms are in fact for your highest good.

The truth is that your life unfolds in unexpected ways, right? Frankly, that's what makes it interesting.

Working the Gap

There is one more useful concept to introduce; that of 'The Gap.' We've already referred to it briefly in the previous chapter. Let's have a closer look ...

The first and most obvious question is, 'What is The Gap?' (Your knee-jerk response might be a clothing store. It is.) Essentially, the gap is the distance between two points...two objects. When talking about the Law of Attraction, we define 'the gap' more narrowly as **the distance between *expectation* and *reality*.**

Put another way, we're talking about the difference between **what you are expecting to happen and what actually happens.** For me, this definition of the gap is the same as the definition of pain. Let me explain what I mean by that with a little anecdote.

Let's say you're wandering along happily in your life, working at a job you don't mind, receiving a salary at the end of every month in compensation for your time and effort. And then, without much warning, you're called into the boss's office and suddenly, without any warning, you're fired. 'The gap' has just appeared in your life.

In this situation, you can see that there is a gap between what you were expecting (that your job will go on as normal) and what has actually happened (that your job as you knew it is over). Now if you're a normal human, this causes you to feel pain. That's what I mean by 'the gap is pain.'

Let's continue gap hunting. Perhaps you're wandering along in your life, ambling towards your forties, and everything is looking pretty much business as usual. Out of the blue, you're asked to do a health check for a new insurance policy. That's not too unusual, and as such it's no problem. You go along to the doctor's office where you're squeezed, prodded, and poked. Someone jabs you with a needle and takes a little blood for testing. This is all within the comfortable limits of your expectations and as such, it's no problem.

Until the gap turns up. The blood tests turn up positive for diabetes. Now *that's* a problem. You feel your entire body react to the stress... your heart starts racing, your stomach feels acid-y, and your head hurts. Once again the gap between what you're expecting and what actually transpires equals pain.

Of course the gap can also occur in a positive way. That's when you come home and find a new car in the driveway or an unexpected invitation to a fancy restaurant. That stuff is easy to deal with and most people love it! In this instance, what actually happened was *better* than expected. So the gap equals pleasure.

The Gap Is What You Make It

Most of us aren't enlightened enough to see the gap for what it really is. The gap, of course, isn't really pain unless you interpret it that way. It's only when the gap is a bad thing that most people get upset.

The gap is nothing more **than an indicator of the distance between you and your desire**. It's not painful in itself; the pain is simply your interpretation. Another way of saying that more directly is that the pain is created by you. The pain is a reaction to things going differently from the way you expected. Thankfully, it doesn't have to be like that.

Let's look, for a moment, at a typical human response to the gap. When the gap hits, most people stay focused on the pain. They stare into the gap, obsessed, poring over the details of this new unexpected event unfolding in the 'what is' of their life. They react to the gap as if it's a picture of their unchanging reality. In truth, the gap is just *what's happening now*. It is not the past, and nor does it define the future; it's just 'what is.' It's a passing thing, no more than a fleeting moment in your life.

Nevertheless, people experience the gap as if it's the only possible thing that can happen in their lives. They get caught up in the pain which makes them focus even more intently on the gap. I know. Even with all the work I've done using the Law of Attraction, I still do it myself. When the gap hits me, I feel the pain. I examine the gap from all angles and torture myself with my observations.

Let's say I'm in the doctor's office, dealing with those blood test results. If I get caught up in the gap, this will be my internal monologue: "Oh my God, I'm overweight and now I've got diabetes. It says so right here on the blood test. That's science, baby, and you can't go against science. Good grief, it's going to hurt, I'm going to die. I'm going to have to jab myself with a needle every five minutes and I hate needles. And I'm going to get fatter. I'm probably going to get more diseases. I'm on a slippery downhill slope that leads only to a slow, painful, horrible death.'

And on and on. The fear and pain are practically overwhelming. But it gets worse. My brain, now trapped in this place of hurt, starts to freak out and begins a desperate search for answers. 'What will I do? What's going to happen? What should I do? What's going to happen?' My brain becomes the metaphysical equivalent of a chicken with its head cut off, running around the yard of my mind in a panic.

On and on it will go left to its own devices, caught up in its own drama. Unless, thankfully, I remember that *it's only the gap*. It's not reality, it's not my life, it's not my future; it's just what's happening right now.

I choose instead to take the time to look more closely, and to *re-phrase* the gap. If I look at *this* moment and only this moment as I read the terrible doctor's result for example, I feel no pain in this particular moment. **Nothing has happened to me yet.** I feel fine right now. The piece of paper in front of me communicates only one **possible future**. I don't even know if it's true. Shouldn't I get a second opinion? Maybe the blood test was wrong. Maybe, even if it's true, I can do something great about it that will enrich my life.

I realize that perhaps this too is part of the perfect unfolding of life in response to my own desires in response to the Law of Attraction. I think "What if the way things are unfolding are the way they're meant to be." And then I wonder, "Is this the best thing for me?" The answer is, 'Yes, it is,"...every time, in every circumstance.

The trick is to train yourself to **see the gap, through your pain.** See it for what it is. It's sometimes difficult or something that may feel impossible to do that in the moment...but *only* in that moment.

The Past Does Not Equal the Future

Another key to unlocking the joy of life is to realize that *the past does not equal the future.* The past is simply a reflection of the choices you made way back when. The future is a reflection of the choices that you're making now, *in this very moment.*

It's amazing to me how many people look at 'what is,' especially when there's a gap causing pain, and then link it up to the idea that 'what is' drives their life. They look at their past and think, 'It happened that way before, leading to the painful scenario I'm in now, so it's going to happen that way again.'

If we apply this philosophy to the doctor's report, it would generate a stream of consciousness and thoughts such as:

- 'I've always been unhealthy, ever since I was a kid. I'm a goner!'
- 'I'm already fat, I eat badly, I don't exercise enough — and now I'm going to have diabetes too!'

And so on. There's an untold suggestion in our culture that our past equals our future. That what has happened before in our lives will happen again. Fortunately, **the world doesn't work like that**. Instead, it works by means of the Law of Attraction.

Like attracts like. What you think about unambiguously, especially with a repeated focus and emotional charge, comes to you. So next time you're in the gap, try focusing on *what you want* instead of 'what is.' Maybe this event is unfolding perfectly, in which case, what is the silver lining? What unforeseen opportunities and connections does this bring? How could this unusual, unanticipated circumstance better your life? How could this here-and-now moment be not just okay, but something more...something better...like perhaps your saving grace?

Remember, your future is completely up to you to manifest in this moment right now. Whatever you've done, said or thought about in the past is just that. It's the past. You're free to change your focus in *this* new moment and start sending your life in the direction of your new desires.

Using Your Emotions to Build Your Perfect Life

There's a new notch in your knowledge belt. It comes with the work you've done so far and your growing understanding of the importance of silencing Brain Chatter. Now we're going to talk about your emotions -- how you feel, not how you think. Emotions are a highly underrated and often misunderstood tool in the moment to moment journey of a life in conscious alignment with the Law of Attraction.

Most people experience their emotions as a reaction to what's happening in any particular moment in the physical world. If you hear bad news, you become sad. If you get good news, you're happy, right?

If you see a fifty dollar note lying comatose on the ground and no one else is around, what do you do? You pick it up, stuff it in your pocket and smile. You're *especially* happy! This is how most people experience emotions, as **something that happens *to* you** as opposed to **something that comes from *within* you** as an expression of personal choice.

The relationship between emotions and conscious alignment goes even further than that. Many people run their lives **in anticipation of future emotions**. You hear this when people say things like, 'If only I had a million dollars, then I'd be happy' or, 'If only I were promoted to manager, I'd be happy' or, 'If only my father had been more loving when I was growing up, I'd be happy.' There's a sense that one has to have or do something first, and then the desired emotional state will follow.

In fact, the opposite is true.

Your Emotions Are Your Choice

Emotions are an internal choice, not a response to an external situation. You can get bad news (Someone has died) and feel happy (Their suffering is over) or sad (That person isn't here for me anymore). The choice of response is yours. You get good news (I won dinner for two at my favorite restaurant) and feel fantastic (I love eating out) or terrible (I don't deserve this).

In both situations, the choice of *how* to feel is entirely in your hands. Emotions, in the moment to moment context, are simply your **personal interpretation** of events that are unfolding. But emotions can be more. You can use them as a tool in the context of the Law of Attraction.

> *Your emotions are a moment to moment guide*
> *indicating your alignment with your desires.*

Here are a few examples to make this clearer:

- Let's say you have to go to work and you feel like you just don't want to. That feeling is an indicator that there's a big difference between what you're doing and what you want to do.

- Let's say you have $10.00 in your pocket and you feel lousy and frustrated about that because you want $1,000,000.00. That feeling is an indicator that there's a veritable chasm between what you have and what you want.
- Let's say you're running with your dog in the park on a sunny morning and you feel just great. That's an indicator that you're in good alignment with your desire; that you love to run in the park with your dog.
- Let's say that you're getting married or maybe holding your baby's hand for the first time and you feel on top of the world. That's an indicator that you're in excellent, extra-close alignment with your desire.

Emotions, in this context, are and can be used as an indicator. That's not so hard to do on a good day. The trick is to use that awareness on days when you feel terrible. On a 'black' day when your emotions are noticeably negative, you can step back and say, 'Hmm. My negative emotions are an indicator of lack of alignment with my desires. What are my desires again?' This will give you an opportunity to re-clarify your desires so that the Law of Attraction can bring them to you.

Let me explain how I work this in a day to day, practical way.

I imagine a scale from one to ten going left to right.

The left hand side, when the scale is one, is an indicator of feeling absolutely horrible. This is that 'I don't want to go on living, I just don't see the point' place.

- Right in the middle of the scale is five out of ten. This is 'Hey, I'm alive and it's OK'.

- Then on the right, at ten, is ultimate happiness, an almost sacred feeling of touching God, total pleasure that almost exceeds the body's capacity to experience it. It's the magical feeling of a child running around at the park, totally carefree. It's rolling about in a tub of $100.00 bills, knowing these are just your spares. It's holding the hand of the one you love as you walk along a beach at sunset, stopping only to sit down and sip from a bottle of expensive champagne. It's orbiting the Earth when you spent your life dreaming of being an astronaut. It's watching your album go "Number One with a bullet" then having your agent call to see if you wouldn't mind talking to Celine Dion, who's waiting on the other line to discuss a duet. Let's all spend more time there, right?

You'll notice that I spent more time describing what being at 'ten' is like that at anything else. In doing that, I am disciplining my thoughts again, and hopefully guiding your attention too. The Law of Attraction, non-judgemental friend and foe that it can be, responds to what you think about, talk about and do, so it's best to focus on 'ten'. What sorts of things bring you to a 'ten'? Get a detailed picture of them in your mind.

Now, having said it's best to stay focused on 'ten,' I have to admit that I think living my life consistently at that level would burn out my circuits pretty quickly. So here's what I do in practice...

I like to think I spend my life somewhere between seven and eight-and-a-half. That means I'm somewhere between obviously happy and actively excited about what's happening and what's about to arrive.

When I wake up in the morning, I like to 'take my temperature' on the emotional scale and see where I am. My morning routine has evolved into a run-ish walk along the local lake, followed by a meditation (detailed in a previous chapter), followed by a walk-ish run home. I find that when I follow this daily practice, my place on the emotional scale heads over to the right.

Later in the day, I take my emotional temperature a second time and spend time contemplating my desires again, thus re-aligning myself with them. I find that when I make the effort to re-frame my life in this way, I'm constantly heading up the scale to the more enjoyable side. If I'm down, I rephrase my thinking until I'm aligned with my desires again. If I'm up, I go further up the scale. Either way my emotions are the indicator guiding and revealing my alignment with my desires, activating the Law of Attraction in a useful and positive way.

Terrible Is As Terrible Does

How does this apply in life? When you're feeling terrible and you don't do anything about it, you attract more terrible. The trick to stopping that progression is to simply check in on the scale, understand you're feeling bad, and then re-focus on your desires until you're aligned again.

For example, let's say you're at work doing a job you hate. You spill your coffee on your shirt first thing, and then you miss an important meeting when the elevator gets stuck between floors. Next, just as it hits ten o'clock in the morning the photocopier jams. This is the final straw. You were already upset and this just tips you over into mad and frustrated. You kick the copier and go back to your cubicle, thinking dark and homicidal thoughts about your boss.

If you don't do something, and instead just 'stew' in your own anger, then the Law of Attraction will bring you more of the same, right? More thoughts and ideas of how bad things are and how they'll never change. But what if, instead of remaining mired in the emotional quicksand in that way, you simply identify your spot on the emotional scale? Like this...

'Oh, hey, I'm at 2 out of ten. That's not useful. I want to feel good. I want to be over there at 3 out of ten. What kinds of things could I think about to get me there?' One answer might be to take a five minute break and start thinking about...or writing down...or talking with a co-worker about... your desires.

'You know, I'm looking forward to going kayaking on Saturday, so it's nice to know we don't work on the weekends,' or, 'You know, I love getting paid every month so that I never have to worry about rent or food, and I still have some left over!', or, 'You know, I love hanging out with all my friends at work, they're a good gang.'

Let's say this 'exercise' brings you to level three on the one-to-ten scale. Maybe with some additional effort, you can raise that to a four out of ten. Like this...

'I want to buy a house, and this job is a great way to get there. If I can stick it out for another twelve months, I'll have enough for a deposit' or 'I want to be a CEO and this job is going to look great on my resume, plus it has loads of opportunity for advancement.'

The Law of Attraction will, as certainly and non-judgmentally as gravity, bring you more thoughts and ideas aligned to your desires. Now your brain is focused on the question of how to feel better and better. And *it will, with the assistance of the Law of Attraction, find the answers.*

Interestingly enough, most people can tell you exactly where they are on this emotional scale without having to think too much. It's one of those times where your first, intuitive answer is usually right. Try asking someone 'Hey, on a scale of one to ten, if one is feeling terrible and ten is feeling awesome, how are you feeling right now?'

Sadly, though most people can identify their emotional state, they don't realize that they are in control of that state. They believe their emotions simply 'happen' to them as a result of what is happening around them. Don't *you* be one of them!

Rather than seeing yourself as a victim of your emotions, it is better to use your emotions as an indicator of where you are. Leverage them as the best possible tool to help you align with your desires, thus helping the Law of Attraction bring you everything you want.

Feeling Better

Now let's talk about another situation where you're in the lower half of the emotional scale. What I mean here is that you are, in a particular moment, feeling less than fantastic. You're feeling worried, stressed or maybe even deeply unhappy and depressed.

At this point, you're probably not having any fun at all. I tend to hate feeling less than fantastic, which is pretty silly, because these feelings are an essential part of life.

Once I'm in this unhappy place, my mind's first response is, 'I want to get the hell out of here. I hate feeling these feelings!' I tend to go to great lengths to avoid having these feelings, but there's no need to. It's a good thing to have them in your life from time to time, just not always. Without knowing depression, how would you recognize joy? There's a lovely contrast that you have to experience to really understand.

The other thing I find, and here's the critical point, is that when I'm feeling in the 0-5 range and trying madly to climb out, I'm generally **making really bad decisions** about how to do that. When you're low emotionally you're simply not clear, not inspired, and not creative. Or at least not *as* inspired, creative or clear as you are when you're at 8, 9 or 10 out of ten.

It's when I'm consistently at 8 out of 10 -- maybe I'm walking on the beach and meditating every day, for example -- that I have my best, most inspired ideas.

So when you're in that lower range of emotions, feeling things like despair, frustration, sadness, don't struggle, don't kick. Don't take panicked action to make yourself feel better. It won't work. You cannot *make yourself feel better*. You cannot avoid feeling the feelings.

What you can do, however, is allow yourself to feel the feelings... and go through them to the other side. Just give it some time! You'll feel better again because **it's human nature to come back into balance**, once you actually admit to, own and feel the feelings you're trying so hard to avoid. And why not try that process we just went through above?

So if you're feeling like something the cat dragged in, don't worry and fret that you can't figure out how to get out of that place. Instead, just *stay* in that place. Give it time, go through it, come to the other side, and emerge naturally.

There now. Don't you feel better?

The Answer is NOT Blowing in the Wind

It was not until I was 21 and finishing up college that I got the urge to live my life in a more deliberate, conscious and intentional manner. Before then, in the more happy-go-lucky days of my 'youth' (translation: before I was 20), I thought 'planning' was a four-letter word. A euphemism for, 'Having a really bad time'.

Had anyone told me that planning was the missing link that would make my dreams come true, would bring me the perfect relationship, financial abundance and humungous unbounded heaps of ecstatic joy, I'm not sure I would have listened. Perhaps. And my early years would have been very different, indeed.

Unfortunately, no one ever did tell me about the power of planning. It wasn't taught in school, at least not where I got my education, not in kindergarten…or middle school…or high school.

With no one to show me how a life lived deliberately could be a life free of want, I preferred to think that it was better to move through life 'organically,' moving wherever the prevailing winds blew me. And boy, did they blow me around. I was constantly moving. I mean *really* moving. I don't think I lived in the same place for more than six months during the four years I spent at college.

There was constant movement in my wallet, too…an unnerving fluctuation in the amount of money that I had, my income level dipping and rising every other month unpredictably. Not a fun way to live!

In other words, my wandering life reflected my wandering focus, which was constantly changing in response to whatever I saw before me. **I lived life in a reactive state.**

I try not to be too hard on myself because in many ways, I think that's what your late teens and early twenties are all about; constant change. Those formative years are about trying a little bit of this and a little bit of that on the road to discovering who you are. In that sense, those years are loads of fun. You get to taste a little of everything from the smorgasbord of life.

I certainly got a taste…of living with plenty and then living with lack, of 3-star restaurants and having to buy a bag of potatoes to eat for the week. I got to try out a bunch of different relationships to see what they were all like. I had a widely contrasting set of experiences from which I was able to build a comprehensive list of likes and dislikes that define me to this very day.

All in all, those experimental days are wild and fun. So I enjoyed them perhaps a little longer than I should have until the curtain was rising on my post-college years and I finally said, 'Enough'.

A Passion for Planning

During my senior year, my business-savvy father made me an offer I couldn't refuse. He said he would spot me the admission fee if I would attend a Tony Robbins one-day seminar with him. My father is an extremely hard-working, career-oriented sort of fellow, and he was keen to get me focused that way too.

We went along to this conference together. It was amazing. It was more like a rock concert than a business seminar! I can still remember Tony's vibrant, passionate presentation style and his intense, visible desire to do good in the world. That resonated strongly with me. Tony's humanistic philosophy alone was an excellent influence and well worth the price of the ticket, although it wasn't advertised in that context on any of the brochures.

The one-day seminar with Tony was the turning point in my relationship with planning. All of a sudden it seemed like planning was an essential tool on my life path, without which I was going nowhere fast.

Going nowhere fast, you understand, is where most of my college buddies were going *by choice* and I enjoyed the aimlessness of it with them for a while. I just didn't want to spend the rest of my life in limbo...floating... disconnected. I realized that I had strong emerging intentions around wealth, possessions, relationships and life experiences. I had powerful emerging desires that were going to take a lifetime to achieve.

It seemed from one day to the next that I got completely and thoroughly inspired to living a more conscious, planned life. Quite literally as though someone had turned on a switch and flooded me with energy.

Shortly thereafter, I started to map out my life in a series of **mind-map diagrams**. I covered the walls with butcher's paper scrawling out the details of what I wanted. I think it may have looked a little crazy to my friends and family.

I didn't have any real explanation for it, but I noticed that just by having a specific plan in place, my life had started to really take off. I was unfamiliar with the concept of the Law of Attraction at the time, although I was already working according to its principles. Luckily I didn't have to know about the Law of Attraction in order for it to work on my behalf.

I had always strongly believed that mapping out your life would box you in and give you fewer options for living since you would be limiting your life experience to what was on the page. But I learned that the opposite was true. All of a sudden, 'boxed in' by plans, I was getting much more done in much less time.

This in turn gave me loads more money, loads more friends, and loads more spare time (all of which were among my early desires). With more money, friends, and time I had more options for living.

It didn't take long for me to get addicted to these extraordinary results. My peers didn't really understand or resonate with what was going on, but that wasn't a huge problem. Graduation Day came; I said good-bye to college friends and college life and moved into the business world. I took to corporate life like a fish to water. These were my kind of people, committed to results via a strong planning process. In the business world, people didn't refer to the Law of Attraction. They didn't call it a Life Summit. Their term was 'Strategic Business Plan.'

You wouldn't dream of starting a business without a plan, would you? And yet people navigate their whole personal lives without a clue as to where they're going or how to get there. Unbelievable.

Then I went to live in California. It was there that I learned about the Law of Attraction, and yet again, my life intensified and sped up and got better in exactly the ways I had wished for.

What it comes down to, I think, is that once you've decided what you want in life, you want to get there as quickly and directly as possible.

And for that, you need to plan.

- Want to make a bunch of money? Your unenlightened boss at the 7-11 isn't focusing his energies on making *you* a millionaire. Get yourself a plan.

- Do you want excellent physical health? Don't expect it to magically transfer itself into you as you sit like a potato in the squishy depths of your couch with your hand in a bag of tortilla chips. Get yourself a plan.

- You want a great relationship? It's not going to happen if you blunder through life, hoping to run into that 'special someone' at the next nightclub/pub/random party. Get yourself a plan.

Wealth...health...to love and be loved. Most of us have pretty similar desires to the ones I've just outlined. And, if you're a parent, then you have another excellent set of goals. You most likely want your kids to be happy and healthy, to enjoy a slice of peace and quiet now and then, and to have enough money so that braces, college, and anything a child could want or need is taken care of.

My desires were coming into reality the more I planned for them. And so, one way or another, I became addicted to planning *because I became addicted to the results.*

I couldn't find any courses, continuing ed classes or seminars at the time that were specifically about life planning, so I listened to seminar tapes and read as many books as I could find. And then I began to put those ideas into practice.

Some great new friends of mine turned out to be interested also, so we started doing sessions together. We were coaching each other by helping one another keep consistent, focused and unambiguous thoughts. It was the birth of the Life Summit...only I didn't realize it.

While I'd been 'doing my thing,' my elder brother had already completed an economics degree and moved into strategic planning for a living. We met up in Italy, would you believe, and did a week-long Life Summit planning session walking through the forests along old dirt roads.

And that brings me to here and now...which is the most wonderful place to be.

I've had some pretty outrageous desires in my life; some pretty audacious dreams. In fact I figure if I'm not doing something that scares me a little, then I'm just not living!

I've dreamed of

- Writing albums and having them released
- Writing books and having them published
- Taking a one man show on a National tour
- Writing and hosting a Nationally broadcast TV show
- Helping the world into greener, more environmentally friendly practices

As these desires have formed, I've used the Life Summit process to plan them out, and **they've all come true**. The Life Summit process has enabled me to form consistent, focused and unambiguous thoughts on a daily basis. In this way I've been able to leverage the Law of Attraction in my favor and I'm glad to say I've realized every single one of these desires in a space of less than ten years.

You can have anything in the world that you want *as long as you know what you want.* The Life Summit process brings that vision into your life in an unambiguous, consistent way. It is a very powerful process, aligned with strong **universal principles** and all I can say is that *it works.*

I hope this chapter and the story of fulfilling my desires has helped you to generate your own urge to plan coupled with your own urge to work with the Law of Attraction. And if it has, there's nothing left to do but to go deeper into the Life Summit process.

The Life Summit –
6 Steps to Everything You Desire

Once or twice a year, with great reverence and depth of purpose, a swathe of limousines pulls up outside my house, complete with CIA-looking security guards, disgorging their VIPs into my discreet home office for an international summit of utmost importance. This summit meeting is so hush-hush that it's not reported in the press; it's so secret that you've probably never heard about it before.

But I'm going to spill the beans. This high-level confab is TLS: Tim's Life Summit, and it's bigger and more important than OPEC, G8, and the Miss Universe Pageant combined.

International Summit of Utmost Importance to YOU

OK, so perhaps I'm embellishing on the facts a bit. In truth, there are no limousines or security guards. No foreign dignitaries and no foreign policy-making. I made that up.

What's real, however, is that my TLS is an ISUI, an International Summit of Utmost Importance (Sounds very Lemony Snicket, doesn't it?). And by the way, Tim's Life Summit isn't just held once a year, either. After all, what could be more important than the mapping out and implementation of your own life? Do you *really* want to wait 12 months between strategic planning sessions?

Every year I read about the big summits held in glamorous places around the world, hosting the world's top financial powers, religious orders and political heads of state. They're surrounded by gates, fences and, usually, protestors. They make big picture decisions that will affect the lives of millions, sometimes billions, over cucumber sandwiches and tea. At least that's how I imagine it.

They decide the funding of the world's economies, which governments will rise and which will fall; they make financial, religious and political policies that seem so removed from my own small life as to appear completely irrelevant.

And they are.

They're not only irrelevant to my daily life, they're completely unimportant despite all the attention they get on the news.

The headlines should read, 'Tim decides to take train to work instead of car on Day 3 of the Summit of Tim' or, 'Tim focuses on making his first million on Day 5 of the Summit of Tim'. And yet, somehow, the headlines don't pay any attention to the minutiae of my life, creating the misleading impression that these details aren't important.

What if, instead of being on the outside looking in to the gatherings of others, I held my *own* high-level Summit, attendance restricted to the most important people in my own life? A special Summit just for me, held regularly, to decide the emotional, economic, physical, financial, spiritual, religious and other important facets of my own life. To reflect upon the past as a guide to the future, to make decisions, with great precision and most of all, to bring focus and clarity to the most important desires in my own life.

What could be more important?

Nothing, of course. The Life Summit process is exactly that. It's the Summit of You. The most important Summit that could ever be held and you don't even have to travel to Geneva.

Enough talk. Let's get onto the Life Summit itself. Read on, and this process, these dreams and adventures will be yours too.

Intuitively Speaking

The Life Summit Process is designed to transform the answer to one simple question from something foggy, cloudy and amorphous into something clear, focused and unambiguous.

So let's get back to the question that is at the core of the Law of Attraction, 'What do you desire?'

When you were young, answering that question was easy, remember? You always knew, moment to moment, what you wanted. You wanted to watch TV or go for a bike ride or eat some chocolate. You were also very intuitive and immediate about what you *didn't* want. You didn't want to go to swimming lessons, you didn't want to clean up your room, you didn't want to do your homework, you didn't want to go to school, and you sure as heck weren't going to eat spinach, no matter what Popeye said. Easy!

That kind of easy, **natural intuitive flow** becomes muffled for most people as they grow older. Why? The answer is actually very easy. Your intuition becomes less and less clear over time because

> You get rusty and out of practice

> You let your left brain, that analytical, empirical, scientific side, make all the decisions.

Why do we go down this 'unnatural' path? Because you're trained to do so. We're taught to act on what we *think* over what we *feel*...to place logic over all else.

Here's a real life example. When you're asked to explain a multi-million dollar budgeting loss as the marketing manager for a large company, which is going to look better when you say it to the board

> 'The decision leading to the loss was based on market share statistics, a $25,000 worth of empirical research and the latest information available on market trends' (Left-brain logic)

> 'I don't know why we lost the money. We spent it because it *just felt right*' (Right-brain intuition)

Obviously the second phrase that deals with the intangible makes you look bad. It's illogical and that's not good in big business...and not that good anywhere else, either.

Learning that 'logic rules' begins when we're very young. As a child, you learn that you're more likely to spend the day in bed watching TV and being served by your mother if you say

> 'Mother, my temperature is up by four degrees, my heart-rate is accelerated and I have spots. This leads me to conclude that I have a fever. Do you concur?'

instead of

> 'Mommy, I feel icky and kind of weird. I think there
> may be a dragon in my tummy or maybe a bee flew
> into my nose. Can I stay home?'

This is a world of computers, of logic and cold, hard facts. In response, intuition is trained right out of you. They beat it out of you at home... at school...in the sandbox...and at the office. And as you become older, you no longer look to your intuition for guidance. Instead, you base your answers on cold, hard facts since they tend to be received more favorably.

It is science and reason that dominate our world over intangible 'gut feelings.' Most people, therefore, as a perfectly sensible response to the culture around them, choose reason over intuition. Put another way, all but the gutsy few stop trusting their guts.

And so, your guts get out of practice. Your intuition gets quieter and quieter until one day you can't hear it at all. And that is a sad, sad day, the more so that it comes and goes unnoticed.

You're being asked to do exactly the opposite of what most people normally do. We're asking you to **abandon reason**. (It sounds daring, doesn't it?) We're asking you to throw caution to the wind. We're asking you to turn a deaf ear to all of that left brain thinking and listen exclusively to your guts.

Get back in the Go with Your Gut game, people! Why? Because intuition, imagination and wild, crazy ideas are where the joy is. They're where the juice in life is hidden. It's in your right-brain that you'll find the joyous answers to the question 'What do you want?'

It should come as no surprise, therefore, that the first work you do in your Life Summit revolves around wild dreams, blue sky thinking, intuitive illogical connections and how you feel when you have no fear of being judged. We want to know what that inner child of yours really wants when you let it out of its cage for a while.

If your 'heart of hearts' could speak, this Life Summit session would be the metaphysical equivalent of taking dictation from your soul.

A Note about Wild Dreams

As a child, do you remember the one question that adults and other kids asked you over and over and over? In my life, that question was, 'What do you want to be when you grow up?' While the answer changed frequently, I was always ready with a response:

> 'I want to be a fireman'
> 'I want to be a forest ranger'
> 'I want to be a spaceship captain'
> 'I want to be King'

I never said my answers were sensible, just that they were clear to me. In fact, most children have clarity on *all* aspects of their perfect life. They know things like

> 'I want to have a million dollars'
> 'I want to win the Olympics'
> 'I want to live in a big house with a pool which has crocodiles in it'

It's this kind of unrestrained, imaginative and irrational clarity that *we must have* in order to move forward. So if your dreams are wild, don't train to tame them. Enjoy them for what they are: unfettered, unbridled...but far from impossible!

The Golden Ball

At this juncture, it's as good a time as any to explain a little Life Summit **jargon.**

Imagine, for a second, that as a child you had a clear notion of what your perfect life would look like. Imagine that you knew every detail of what you'd do, who you'd be with, where you'd live, how much you'd earn, what you'd believe in. Imagine that you knew *everything*. Now imagine that this perfect life could be represented as a *perfect golden sphere* floating out in front of you ready for you to grab. Have you visualized the shiny golden ball, floating there in all of its perfection, representing your perfect life vision? Good.

What happens for most people as they grow up is that reality starts to get in the way. All of a sudden that golden ball is a little further from you and maybe a little smaller too. It's the perfect life you'll get *after* you've finished school. It's the perfect life you can have *if* you graduate top of your class at college. It's the perfect life you can have if you *scale it down a little* and accept your limitations. Sound reasonable?

Sound familiar?

Tarnished

Bit by bit, you no longer perceive your golden ball as your birthright; it becomes something you can have *conditionally* -- if and as you jump through an ever more complicated set of hoops. And so these challenges and compromises that life hands you start to change your perfect golden ball into something a little less perfect and a little less golden.

Then fear starts to creep in and your golden ball starts to really get tarnished and even more remote. All of a sudden you find yourself separated from your golden ball by a chasm. So you build a mental rope bridge across the chasm, kind of like the one in the movie 'Indiana Jones and the Temple of Doom'. Under your precarious bridge are rapids churning the river thousands of feet below. And if the rapids don't get you, the hordes of hungry crocodiles will!

Metaphorically speaking, the rope bridge represents your own personal **tightrope of life.**

Your fears tell you that one single mis-step in life means you'll fall, smashing yourself into a mangled pulp as the crocs get busy on what's left of you. Beware! Everything is fine as long as you keep your job, but if you don't... Everything will keep going nicely as long as you don't step out of line with your boyfriend or girlfriend or spouse or business partner or parents or friends, but if you don't.... Everything is cool as long as you stay away from drugs, smoking, fatty foods, salty foods, the wrong part of town, crossing the road and taking a bath with a toaster in the room, but if you don't...

The fear of 'if you don't' creates tremendous stress in life as you imagine what could go wrong and do your best to make sure it doesn't. It's exhausting.

So how does your beautiful golden ball look now? A lot like a lump of lead, I bet.

Now, from where you stand, that golden ball looks a long way away. The perfect life you imagined as a child seems...well, childish. Sure, you wanted to have a million dollars, but now that's impossible. It's just not how your life turned out, right?

So you scale down your dreams. Maybe you should just go for owning your home, which seems more do-able. Or if that seems too hard what with the price of property doubling in the last five years in the housing boom, just renting would be fine. Then you ask yourself "What's the smallest budget we could live on? And can the government help us in some way? We're living hand to mouth!"

Piece by piece, most people start to go through a process of compromising their dreams as a response to what's going on around them... to "What is." As your perfect life is reduced and reduced, as that golden ball gets smaller and smaller, that dangerous chasm becomes narrower and narrower until it disappears altogether. So in a sad way, that feels like a good thing.

You can scale your life down until it's impossible to disappoint yourself. You can pay attention to your fears, accepting their version of reality, and choose your actions accordingly until your life is totally safe. Now, thankfully, you can reach your golden ball with a single step.

There are no risks, only safety. The rope bridge is completely gone along with the raging river and the crocodiles below. Wow. Thank goodness. There's only one problem: **This is not the life you were born to live.**

This is not your soul's soaring vision! This is a life of compromise; a life lived half-asleep as you focus on avoiding all the potential dangers and possible pitfalls. For as you remove all the potential downsides, you remove all the potential upsides also.

I say, Bring on the rope bridge! Bring on the rapids! Bring on the hordes of crocodiles — after all, maybe they're vegetarians!

I'm inviting you...urging you to focus on defining your most perfect, shining, enormous, overwhelming, impossible and unlikely golden ball without compromise. It's absolutely revisiting your childhood clarity, your audacious and unlimited vision of possibility. Now is the time to **throw off all your fears and dream it up big!** Dare I say it: Go ahead and have a ball!

What Do You Want?

In order to make the Law of Attraction work, you need to be clear about your desires. That's why we've been talking so much about that one simple question, 'What do you want?' Now let's make it a little more interesting by extending it a little and ask **'What do you want in your perfect life?'**

This question will be the stepping stone that you will use to cross over from 'dreaming' to 'living' your desires. Actually, it's one of several stepping stones in The Life Summit Process. Other helpers include serious things like mathematics (to help you divide and conquer your long term desires) and silly things like junk food (to help you keep your inner child entertained and engaged).

The nice thing about stepping stones is they make it easy to get from one place to another. So instead of taking a giant step from the here-and-now to your perfect future...and possibly start to drown in the details of 'How will I get there?"...

Let's take a smaller step to a closer stone and ask:

**'What does your perfect life look like
ten years from now?'**

Step #1 - Your Perfect Life in Ten Years

You may be wondering why I'm taking a quantum leap and asking this question about a time so far into the future.

In talking about the future, the left-brain checks out because there's nothing for it to do. Good! There's nothing here for the left brain to do, so it *should* leave. Anything happening ten years from now is a dream, a lark which has nothing to do with the cold hard reality of 'What is."

We all know that ten years from now pretty much anything could happen, right? There could be huge breakthroughs in technology changing transport, medicine, business and entertainment. There could be bull markets and recessions. There will be volcanoes and hurricanes and sweet sunny days. Flesh-eating zombies from another planet could try to take over the planet. Who knows what the face of the planet will look like in ten years?

By the same token, who knows what the landscape of your life will look like in ten years? So invite your left brain to leave the room and reassure it that it can go in peace, knowing that we're going to have great fun talking about unreasonable dreams, unlimited desires and the prospects of a *soul gone wild.*

Now as this book is being written, it's 2009. So if you're reading it and doing your Life Summit work in 2009 you would write in the middle of the page 'My Perfect Life in 2019', dated ten years from now, yes?

Ooh. Juicy. Fun! What would your life look like in the future...ten years from now, when anything is possible? Answer these questions:

- What job would you have?
- How much money would you be earning?
- What would your career look like?
- How is your health?
- What are you doing with friends and family?
- Are you having holidays? If so, how many and where are you going?
- Where are you living?
- What adventures are you having?

Your facilitator is to ask the questions; you're to sit on the comfy couch and answer them. Your facilitator is to write down the answers; you're to eat all the candy and drink all the Red Bull.

Of course, these are only example questions to get you started. There are all kinds of ways to ask the same question again and again from every possible angle:

- What would you be doing, if you could do anything you wanted?
- What are you doing about exercise and nutrition?
- How does your home look?
- What super cool fun things are happening in your life?

Ask and answer these questions and more like them as you explore your perfect life without limits.

Breaking it Down

Some people find it easier to break the 10-Year Page up into a few basic topics, and then filling it out from there. This makes sense in light of associative nature of the brain; once you give it something to start on, it's flying!

If you like this idea, rather than just starting in on your Life Vision 2019, you might start with some broad topics like:

Professional life/career

- ☐ Family life/personal
- ☐ Relationships – spouse/children/social
- ☐ Health/exercise/eating/physical body
- ☐ Spirituality/religion
- ☐ Finances/budgets
- ☐ Possessions/collections
- ☐ Property
- ☐ Life Experiences

- ☐ Fun/enjoyment/leisure time activities
- ☐ Travel/holidays
- ☐ Giving back/charity/community work

Then, having listed and possibly underlined these major topics, you could work your way around the mind map methodically, filling out every strand in detail. Most likely answering this first question alone will take you several hours.

Here are some more linked questions that you might ask and answer on these particular topics:

Professional life/career

- ☐ What job would you like to be doing, if any?
- ☐ Where would you like your career to be?
- ☐ Are you going to be in the job you're in now, or a different one? If so, which job?
- ☐ Are you going to be in the same field you're in now, or another?
- ☐ Will you have won any particular awards or recognition?
- ☐ Will you have secured any raises or bonuses?
- ☐ How will you feel about your job?
- ☐ Who will you be working with?
- ☐ What kinds of people will you be working with?

Family life/personal

- ☐ What will your relationship with your family be like – both your own immediate family (if you have partner/kids) and your extended clan?
- ☐ What will be the significant events in your family?
- ☐ What special annual events are you planning for your family?

Relationships/spouse/children/social

- ☐ What key relationships will you have by 2019?

- ☐ Will you have a wife/husband/meaningful other? If so, what kind of person will that be?

- ☐ How many kids will you have, if any?

- ☐ What kinds of social and professional connections will you have?

- ☐ What kinds of friends will you have and how will you relate to them?

Health/exercise/eating/physical body

- ☐ What kind of body are you going to have?

- ☐ What kinds of specifics could describe your perfect 2019 body?

- ☐ What will you weigh?

- ☐ How will you look?

- ☐ How will you feel?

- ☐ What kinds of things will your body be able to do?

- ☐ What level of fitness will you be at?

- ☐ How will you physically feel?

Spirituality/religion

- ☐ What kind of connection to religion or spirituality will you have?

- ☐ What kinds of spiritual or religious practices will you observe?

- ☐ What kinds of spiritual or religious friends or guides might you be connected with, and how?

- ☐ Will you be part of a particular spiritual or religious community? And if so, how will you participate?

Finances/budgets

- ☐ How much money will you be making?

- ☐ How might this money be coming to you?

- ☐ What kind of money will you have around you, and in what forms? How much in savings? How much in property, stocks, bonds, mutual funds or shares?

- ☐ What kind of money will you have invested and in what kinds of projects?

- ☐ How much money will you be able to spend freely each day, week, month, and/or year?

- ☐ How much money will you contribute to the community?

Possessions/collections

- ☐ What kinds of possessions will you have?

- ☐ How will they look, what will they be like?

- ☐ Where will you keep them?

- ☐ What will you use them for?

- ☐ How will you share them / make use of them?

Property

- ☐ What kind of property will you have?

- ☐ Where will you be living?

- ☐ Will you be renting or owning or a combination?

- ☐ Will you own a house or maybe more?

- ☐ Will you own or mortgage investment properties and if so, what will they be?

- ☐ What property portfolio will you build, if any?

Life Experiences

- ☐ What kind of life experiences will you have?

☐ Will you sky dive, scuba dive or bungee? What kinds of amazing adventures will you have?

☐ What kinds of outdoor dream activities will you enjoy over the next ten years?

☐ What kinds of indoor adventures will you have?

☐ What adventures will you experience on your own, what kinds with your friends and / or family?

☐ What 10 essential things must you do before 2019?

☐ Where will you travel?

Fun/enjoyment/leisure activities

☐ What things will you do regularly and just for fun?

☐ What activities keep you balanced, whole and happy?

☐ What are the top three enjoyable things that you can do on a weekend?

☐ What are the top three enjoyable things you can do after work?

☐ What are the top three enjoyable things you can do during work hours?

Travel/holidays

☐ What will you do on your holidays?

☐ Where will you go on your holidays?

☐ How many holidays will you have and how often?

Giving back/charity/community work

☐ In what ways will you contribute to parties outside yourself, your friends and family?

☐ In what ways will you participate in the community around you locally, in the broader community and globally?

Don't think, just write! Fill the walls with your wild ideas and dreams.

A Note on Being Specific

When you're doing this kind of process, it pays to be **as specific as you can be** about what you want. If you're talking salary, say how much. If you're talking about people, describe them. If you're talking holidays, specify the length, the location and any other details you can fill in.

The thing to avoid, if possible, is describing the 'how.' As we've discussed at length in the first part of this book, we want this process to work *with* the Law of Attraction, not against it. Your job is to focus on what you want. Your job is to entertain clear, focused, unambiguous and consistent thoughts around your desires. This process is all about making those desires clear and focused.

What we want to avoid is describing *how* things are going to happen, since that part of manifesting is *not your job*. It's up to the amazing implacable power of the Law of Attraction to deliver your desires in the form of its own choosing, which often is even more amazing than your own anticipated plan. So avoid focusing on *how* these desires will come to you, just focus on the desires themselves.

Being specific without describing 'the how' is tricky. Let me give you an example here...

During a recent Life Summit focusing on the life of a flourishing rock star, the desire came up 'I want my new album to play on radio station KZZP'. On one level this is lovely and specific. The way this desire was expressed, however, was a little constrictive.

We explored the desire a little and what came out was 'I want my songs to be heard on radio by millions'. This, second desire was less prescriptive. This second expression of the desire allowed radio play across all radio networks not just the one. It was a better expression of desire than the first in that it has **fewer limitations**.

A Note on Self-Facilitation

If you don't have a facilitator, you must self-facilitate during the Life Summit process. That means that in addition to everything else you're doing, you have to keep yourself talking and, on the odd occasion, to banish your left brain from the room.

You'll know when your left brain is peeking in because it usually announces its arrival with the word 'but'. For example, I want a million dollars," says your right brain. *"But* I don't know how it's going to happen' adds the left brain. Or

 - 'I want a super-sexy six foot tall hot blonde vixen as my wife, *but* I'm just hopeless in bars'. Stop arguing for your limitations, you left brain you! Or

 - 'I want to be the chief scientist at NASA, guiding the space shuttle missions into orbit, *but* I don't even have a degree'

 - Tell your left-brain to 'but' out and leave you alone. This is your right brain's time in the sun! This is the time to connect to that part of you that is inspired, creative, fun, flowing, child-like, joyful and completely unreasonable!

Troubleshooting

Most people have lots of fun writing down in great detail how their perfect life should look. You can barely stop them from talking as they get on a roll or into a flow. On the other hand, this can also be difficult. Some people find it difficult to let go and just get silly.

If you're stuck, you might want to turn the question around and ask "What do I NOT want." Most people can talk for ages on what they don't want, which becomes a useful context for constructing a more positive picture later.

For example, as a facilitator, after asking, 'So what don't you want?' you might get answers like

- I don't want to be broke
- I don't want to be unhealthy or to get cancer
- I don't want to be alone
- I don't want to be bored
- I don't want an old bomb for a car
- I don't want to do this same horrible job forever

You can then flip these back, reversing each comment into a new question like

- Okay, you don't want to be broke, so how much money do you want if you could have as much as you wanted?
- Okay, you don't want to be unhealthy and get cancer, so how do you want your body to be?
- Okay, you don't want to be alone, so who do you want to be with?
- Okay, you don't want to be bored, so what sorts of things could you do that would be exciting?
- Okay, so you don't want an old bomb for a car, then what car would you like?
- Okay, so you don't want this same horrible job forever, then what job would you like?

A Page from My Own Book

Here's an example using my own life. It's currently March 2009 so I'm looking at March 2019 for this session. As you might expect, I've done this once or twice before, so it flows pretty easily.

I start by writing, 'Tim in 2019' into the middle of the page.

Next, since I'm already reasonably clear about the main topic areas of my ideal life, I write out these topics in a rough circle around the middle, connecting them with lines and underlining them. Please, don't be as neat as this; I'm just showing off because these maps are for a book!

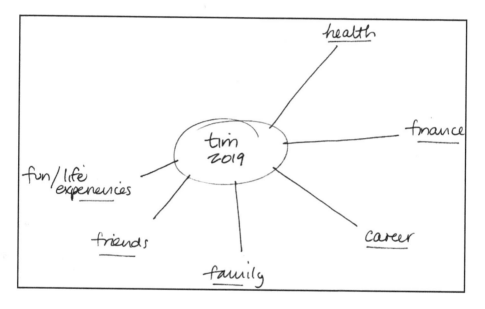

My main topics are health, finance; career, family, friends and key life experiences that I want to have had by the time the clock strikes 2019. I've also left a bit of a space blank at the top of the page. That's useful in case I've forgotten something major.

Without planning it out, just going by feel, I decide to fill out my career and finance stuff first. That's usually fairly top of mind for me. It's probably because one of my major life roles as a father is supporting my family financially. I learned that from *my* dad. So I start there.

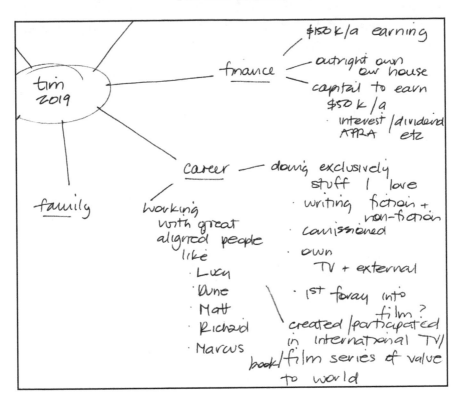

You'll notice that I'm getting increasingly specific here. I'm describing exactly how much money I'm going to be making, that I'm going to outright own my house, and so on. But there's one little bit under finance where I get a little stuck.

My intention is to have enough in various investments that I'm earning $50k from interest, dividends, licensing fees and whatever else. There's a bit of math to do here to figure this out more specifically, but it feels a little too left brain, so I'll leave it until later. For now I'd prefer to keep going while I'm feeling clear and creative.

If you get the feeling that you're blocked on any particular topic like that, **it's best to move on**. Go instead to an area where you're feeling clear and inspired with loads to say. Most likely you'll be inspired to come back later and pick up where you left off in the blocked part.

Okay, I've created links for finances. Now with career I don't really know which company I'll be working for in ten years, or if I'll be working for a company at all! So I focus on which roles I enjoy and other key career components, such as working with great people. I even give a few examples from my current list of friends, so I know what kinds of people I'll be working with.

Next, again in no particular order, I start to link ideas to friends and family.

friends
- be utmost
  close friend
- fun things
  together
- calls/email
  mail
  connection
- mutual support
  + guidance

family
- be utmost
  loving father
- encouraging happy
  Ange + Zak + Finn
    + Baby3
- providing comfortably
  for all inc.
  ideal education
    ↳ steiner?

C...
workin...
with
align...
li...

One way or another, I like to think of myself as a supportive and nurturing friend, so that goes down. I like to make sure that my friends are getting phone calls, emails and the occasional letter to keep the communication going. After all, the relationship is in the conversation, right?! I also like to invite my friends and family around regularly or go to some cool meeting spot, going on what my kids call a 'play date'.

In my opinion play dates should never, ever stop. Why else are you alive?

In my map, I've focused on the roles of friends and family. But I could have specified, 'I'll have 6 close friends, 42 business associates and 10,000 friends on Facebook!' It's all about whatever works for you, personally.

Next there's a note on health or what I term 'my physical body.' In 2019 I'll be 47. Wow! That seems like an advanced age. Just three years away from 50! But however old I am, I plan to have an active, vital, physical and healthy life. So I put that down:

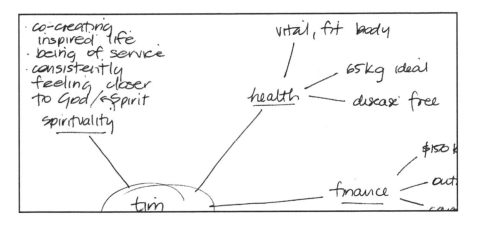

Around about now, as I wax lyrical on life's meaning, I realize that I am, after all, missing an important topic. Some call it religion or beliefs, but I term it *spirituality*.

This is a tricky one for me to express knowing that this is going to be published in a book. After all, spirituality is a pretty personal thing for me. So I ask you to be kind, understanding and right-brain non-judgmental as you continue to read this section.

The easiest aspect of my spirituality to discuss in a way that most people can relate to is my clear desire for a close connection to Spirit. Most would call it God, the Devine or The Universe. I'm also keen to be of service as a lifelong role, not just to my friends and family but to a larger, more global community. So I put that down too.

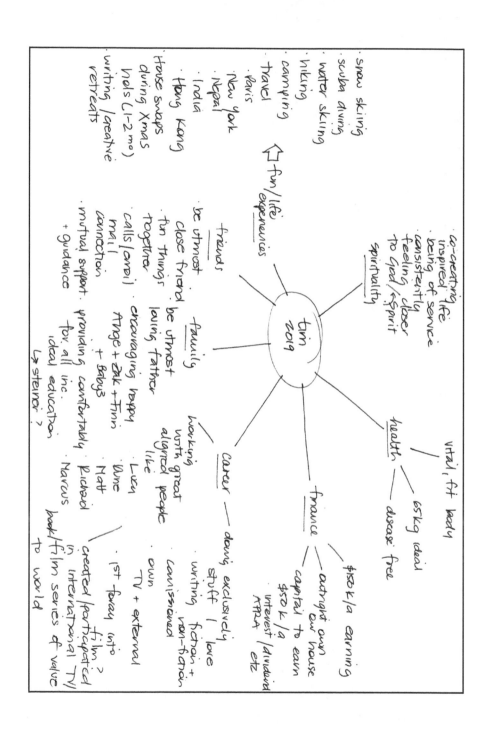

Leaving the heady topic of spirituality, I move on to something a little lighter; the topic of fun!

I consider fun as a top priority in life. So I write down a list off the top of my head of some of the more seriously fun play dates that I count on having in the next ten years. For example, I've been dreaming of revisiting my youth by scuba diving somewhere fantastic like the Great Barrier Reef or Lord Howe Island. Put it down. My wife and I are keen to travel, so I write down our five favorite places.

With fun mapped out for the future, I realize I'm done! Maybe not totally, completely, absolutely done...but done.

At this point, I like to ask myself 'Do you feel about 80% complete?' And if I do, then that's enough. You can never be 100% complete with this process. It's not possible since your desires are changing from moment to moment, let alone across months and years. So now that my mind map is comfortably covering 80% of my ideal life, I give myself permission to stop and move on.

It's definitely not a problem if you miss a few things; you can always jot them down later. I tend to leave my mind maps up on the wall so I can make changes without a problem.

Enjoy Yourself

As you can imagine, most people have trouble fitting their entire life dreams on just the one page. By now I expect you've already filled up several pages with notes and random observations, things to get back to and formative lists. That's why I have nine sheets of paper on the wall, not just the one.

Just to give you a feel for what those other pages might look like, I've broken out one of my topics - 'Career' - for a more detailed look. While you certainly don't *have* to do this, you are welcome to, especially if you have a bit more detail in your mind about how your perfect life is going to be.

I start, then, with a new topic in the middle of the page. Then I map out the topics, as before. Of course you don't have to do it this way. Be organic! It's up to you.

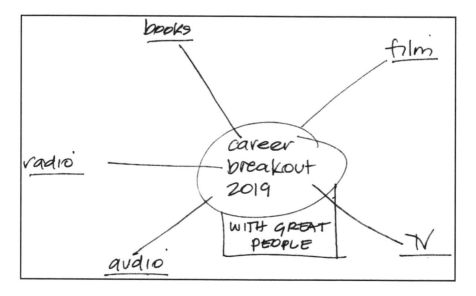

You might notice that I did a little 'drop down' entry under the main bullseye here. That's because I realized that working with great people is *absolutely key* to my career. Without great people I invariably have a horrible time. So a little drop down serves to clarify, at every moment, that key priority for my working life. You can't go wrong striving for clarity, since the Law of Attraction feeds on that kind of detail.

Notice I don't say who these people are by name, just that they're great.

It would be worth going on to define more specifically what makes a person great in my eyes. The definition of 'great people' is different for everyone. For me, it's about being positive, fun loving and life embracing. It's about being talented, passionate and really connected to what you're doing. I make a note of this on another one of my space pages, and then come back to the Career breakout.

Here is my career breakout filled out completely. You know that I've gone through an organic, messy process to get here, so this is just to show you how it wound up.

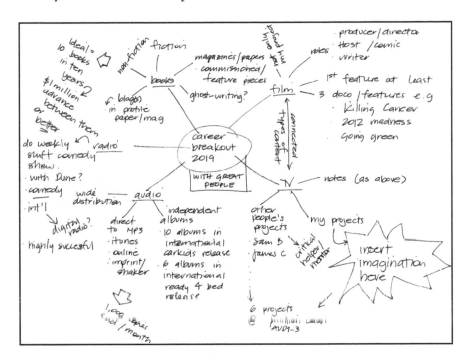

Note that I was again extremely specific when possible. I didn't just write up, 'I want to do some TV projects'; I wrote up '6 TV projects with a budget of at least one to three million Aussie dollars each'. I didn't just write, 'I want to do films', I wrote up the specific roles that I enjoy; executive producing, producing, directing, hosting with a comic tone and of course, writing.

This a good place to make your desires specific and measurable. Having said that, you don't want to start describing *how* these things will come to pass. You'll note I did not write 'I want my show on CNBS, 6pm Tuesdays' because that would be too restrictive...too limiting.

You'll also note a star in the corner with 'Insert Imagination Here' written boldly inside. Inspiration keeps its own timetable. These things hit me when the time is right, as opposed to having ten years worth of creativity laid out neatly already. So I've just put in a little note to hold the space, knowing that the specifics of those projects will turn up in an enjoyable, timely manner.

The 80/20 Rule

If you've been in the business world at all, chances are you've already heard of the 80/20 rule. In the Mind Mapping/Law of Attraction world, it means that you get 80% of your 10-year vision done in 20% of the time. If you then want to get the other 20% of your plan done and perfect, things generally slow down and take much longer...another 80% of your time.

In this case that translates to, say, getting 80% of your vision on the page in the first 2 hours, then needing another 8 hours to complete it.

So don't complete it! You don't need to achieve 100% clarity on where you'll be in a decade. 80% of your vision is plenty to work with. That's why I say that once you feel you've got a solid 80% of your plan up on the wall, you should relax, sit back and move on to the next stages.

To get to the 80% mark might take you an hour, or maybe two. It shouldn't take much longer than that and may take considerably less. In fact, as you do this process over and over during the course of years you'll get quicker and quicker. When you've been mind mapping for a while, you end up **reinforcing your existing vision**, tweaking it in places, rather than starting from scratch every time.

So relax, be easy on yourself, and embrace imperfection. The goal of your 10-Year Map is not to create a vision that is 100% accurate. The idea is to get your vision into words on a page that you can 'share' with your left brain in the next parts of the Life Summit process.

You Deserve a Break Today

And so, walls covered with messy butcher paper mind maps and notes, the crumbs of numerous packs of Doritos littering the floor and several hours later, *Step One is done.*

If you haven't done so already, take a break. Celebrate your success so far. Well done! Your wall is looking messy with creation and imagination. What a cool life you've drawn up!

Go for a walk around the block; have a snack. Do something that takes your mind completely out of this space. When I say completely, I don't mean back to your normal life. I do not mean check your email, your cell phone or mail box for messages of urgency to bring your brain back into your every day. I just mean get some sun or rain onto your face, grab a huge drink of water to re-hydrate, or even sit and meditate!

Just be sure to do something to reset. Take at least half an hour. Then come back, ready to jump into the next part of the process.

Before we leave the first half of the Life Summit process, there are two more points to cover...managing your creative flow and keeping track of it digitally.

Managing The Creative Flow

Ultimately mind mapping should look and sound fairly easy. And really, at its heart, it is. What could be simpler than answering the question 'What do you want?'

Having said that, however, I should expand on the thought and say it's easy *when you're routinely connected* to your creative side, your intuition and your inspiration. If you're not, you may find it valuable to do the exercise above in defining 'What you don't want' first. That tends to open up the creative flow.

If you're still stuck, try to find a buddy to help you through the process as your facilitator. Try someone who knows you quite well already without being invested in the outcome. Find someone who can coax you out of your shell.

If you're still at a loss, why not volunteer to take someone else through the process as their facilitator? You'll learn heaps about how the process works simply by doing it, often learning what you most need to know by showing someone else, and freeing up your own creativity in the process.

Keeping Digital Notes

Lugging around huge swathes of butcher's paper isn't everyone's idea of fun. Certainly not mine. So I use technology to tame those pages. I keep a digital camera with me and take hi-res snapshots of every page at the end of the day. I then throw them onto my PC and if I really need a record, print them out small on my desktop printer. If I want to, I can send them to people at lo-res via email. Everything is flexible when you go digital on this!

One way or another, these pages are not just decorative. We're going to use them as we go and then periodically through the year, so hang on to them in one form or another.

You're Right On Schedule

Congratulations! You've now done what most people consider the 'hardest' work in this book. You've done the deep soul searching required of you. You've brought definition to a heretofore foggy and amorphous vision of your perfect life. Well done!

And admit it: it was fun, wasn't it? It's a little addictive, too. You'll know you're on the right track because you'll be feeling excited and energized too!

Good. By now you should have a good sense of what your perfect life looks like in glorious detail. It is this clear vision that will actually bring that life barreling towards you by means of the Law of Attraction.

The trick is to focus on this vision consistently and unambiguously, *without doubts or conflicts*.

With that in mind we're going to invite your left brain back into the room and put it through its paces. As we've said already, your left brain is all about process, about results, about structure and math. So we want this part of you to come in and create a series of **realistic, structured plans** to bring your perfect life into the real world.

Let's just be clear here, we're not asking your left brain to tell us *how* it will all happen. That's the Law of Attraction's job, organizing the connections, coincidences, resources and inspirations necessary to manifest your desires.

Your left brain is simply to sharpen the focus.

Buckle up your seatbelt. We're going to be moving fast!

Step #2 - Mapping Your 5-Year Plan

Now, taking a fresh sheet...and **keeping your ten-year plan within view**...create your bullseye with My Life in 2014' (or whatever the date is five years from now). Then, working from your ten-year plan, write out the exact same topics, underlining and linking each to the centre.

Staying with the Life Summit mapping example from my own life that I used as an illustration earlier, my 5-year plan would look like *this*.

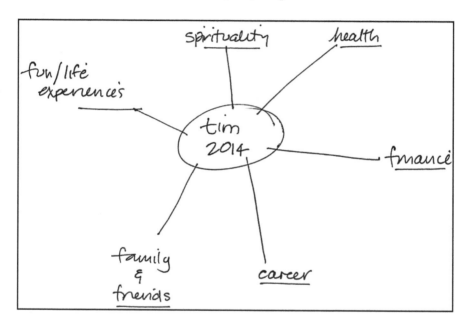

Now working around the page topic by topic, let's create a comfortable **half-way point** in your ten year vision. Not all things are going to split in two easily, so just use this halving idea as **a guide rather than a rule.**

Let's start with finance. I have a goal to be pulling down an annual income of $150,000 each year by 2019. No problem there. That sounds great!

Now, to get my 2014 goals from my previously defined 2019 goals, I halve this number to $75,000 per annum. Well done, left brain. But wait. Within the logic of left-brain, there's a place for intuition and feeling here. $75,000 is 'correct' according to the math but does it *feel* right?

Actually, no, it doesn't. It's close, but not quite right. The point is that I'm not starting from an income of $0.00 per annum. I've been working for half my life already. Also I don't want to wait ten years to earn that much. I'd like to get there sooner, so I'll just write $150,000 per annum up again. That's where I'd like to be in 5 years. Good! That feels better.

According to my ten-year vision, I'll own my home outright. Great. This one is easy. If I completely own my house by 2019, then I want to have paid back half of my mortgage by 2014. Good. I make a note about that.

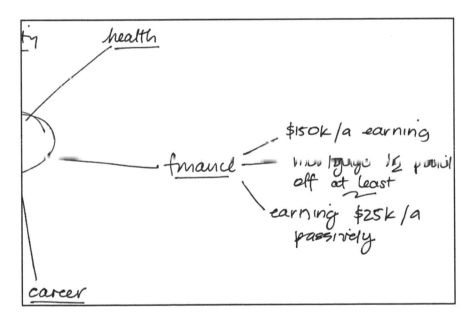

All right. The next thing I notice is that several of my ten-year vision points are things I want to do straight away, so I copy up or just make a note referring back to the 2019 plan.

My health is a good example of something that I don't want to wait a decade to enjoy. I want physical vitality, energy and focus now! I also modify my weight goal to a halfway point, which may or may not have a perfect nutritional basis, but which *feels* right. So I write it down and I thank my intuition for its input.

Your Feelings Are Like Post-It Notes

That's a key point here. While the left brain is in the room and the right brain has pretty much left at this point, your feelings are around at all times. Remember earlier when I said that each side of your brain can leave 'notes' for the other? This is one of those instances.

By all means pay attention to your feelings and intuition as you work the chart, making sure that all of these goals feel good. Don't worry too much about whether they feel *possible,* that's not your job. Leave the 'how' up to the Law of Attraction, remember?

Just make sure that these are things that you genuinely want. In order to be certain, you must pay close attention to your feelings.

Here's what we've mapped so far:

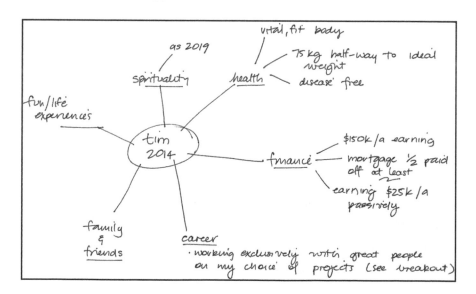

Terrific. Do you see how this is working? Logically, working bit by bit, we're bringing a huge, ambitious, impossible looking life dream back into the realm of day-to-day reality. This is where the left brain likes to stretch out, relax, and enjoy.

Oops! I've just spotted a problem here. Under 'Health' I've written 'disease free'. Now the Law of Attraction, as you know, doesn't see the difference between 'I want to be disease free' and 'I want to be diseased'. It just sees 'disease.' I don't want to attract disease to me in any way shape or form, so I'm going to re-frame that desire into something more positive, with no negative connotations. The better note would be, 'I want to be full of vitality and juice!'

Now I have just two topics to go...or so it seems. However, I've learned that I often come up with a totally new topic at this point. Do I put it on the map? Sure! Of course! And so should you! You can either jam it in here or go back and add it to your ten-year vision. With your highly associative brain you'll be coming up with new ideas all day; the key is to embrace and capture them without judgment...*even when your left-brain is in charge.*

For my map, I came up with a new idea under 'family and friends' which I integrated for simplicity's sake, since my close friends are like family to me. I had the idea that I'd like to remember my loved ones' birthdays more carefully, perhaps with a card or an email or even some kind of party. So I wrote that in. I also had the idea that I could make the effort to do some 'random acts of kindness' for my friends and family to make them feel loved and special each year. Plus, it would be great fun!

Thinking about sharing the love, I got creative and wrote up two new breakout charts defining what I meant by those two ideas.

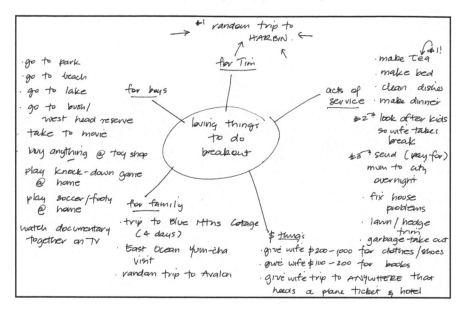

As you might remember from my endless repetition – which underscores the importance of this idea – we want to have specific, unambiguous, well defined ideas. That's why I do my best to quantify each desire as much as possible.

In the case of my right-brain idea to commit random acts of kindness for my friends and family, my left-brain immediately wanted to get into the act and know what those acts were. So to calm my left-brain, I've mapped out specific ideas. The good news is that even if I don't stick exactly to this chart, the act of defining these acts will bring these kinds of things towards me via the Law of Attraction.

Good. Now, swinging back from the breakout we return to the five year plan filling in the last topic on my chart; fun life experiences. In this case I had listed a dozen or more cool things that I want to do in the next ten years on my 2019 plan. So I simply **select around half of them** to include in the next five years. Of course, being me, I come up with a couple of new ones as I go. This is a good thing, so go with it!

Here's how we land with the five year chart complete for now.

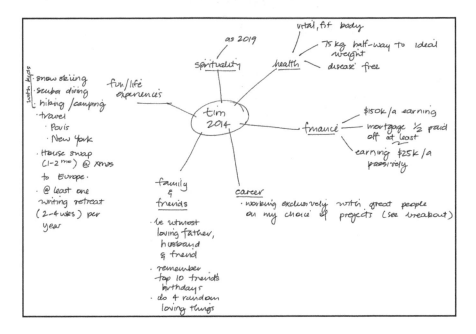

Step #3 – Mapping Your One Year Plan

By now you've probably figured out the next step; to create a one year plan outlining your intentions and desires for the next twelve months. Again, don't get too stuck on how it's going to happen. Resist the temptation to wrap your mind around every minute detail and step. *This is not your job.* Leave the 'how' to the Law of Attraction. Right now your job is to get breathtakingly clear and focused on what you want.

Take a fresh sheet of paper, moving others to more remote areas of the wall / windows / surrounding area if you need the space.

Write 'My Life in One Year' in the middle of the page, surrounding it again with the same topics. Or, in this case, I wrote 'Tim 2010' which means the same thing! Again, since I'm writing this in 2009, this is a 2010 plan and will look something like *this*.

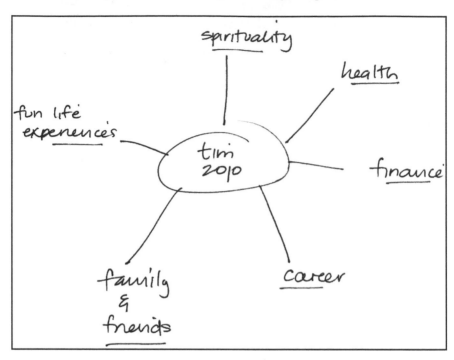

I imagine that by, now, you're really getting into the swing of things and know what you need to do. But just to clarify: this is the time to simply take your ten year plan and 'divide it' by ten, or your five year plan and 'divide' by five. Why is the word 'divide' in quotes? Because this isn't just math, it's math guided by emotion.

For example, in my ten year plan I had an annual income of $150,000. Clearly I want to earn more than $15,000, one tenth of that, this year. I want the whole $150,000 per annum right away, so I write that down. Remember, it's not your job to figure out the 'how', leave that to the Law of Attraction. Just get a clear, unambiguous focus on what you want.

So here's the finished one year vision,

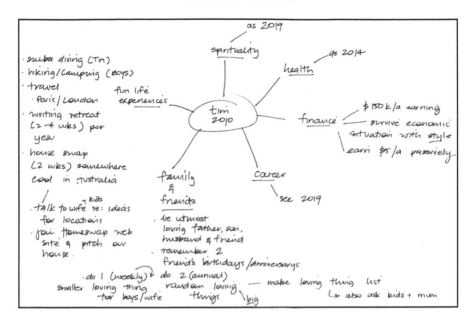

You'll notice that some things have been scaled down from the ten-year plan by a factor of ten, and some not. I've let myself be guided by my feelings; by asking the question 'What feels good for 2010?'

Another small note; as I wrote out this ten year plan, I continued to come up with more and more detail. I realized that I wanted to split my random loving acts into small ones that I could do weekly and big ones that might come only once or twice a year. And just for fun, I tried some out on my wife, making dinner for the family, cleaning up the kitchen completely and sending the wife out for a coffee hour while I looked after the kids. What can I say — it works!

Good. Right about now you should have a ten year vision, a five year vision and a one year vision. Can you guess where we're going to go with this next? You guessed it; we're going to break it down *even further.*

The time has come to switch over to your left brain and crank up your PC. We're going to map out your one-year vision, knowing that it represents the first of five years that make up your five-year vision...which is in turn the halfway point to the ten-year vision...which is your perfect life!

Let's start by converting your one-year vision into something a little more scientific; an **Excel spreadsheet**. Of course you can do this in any software you choose. I like to use Excel for this. In Excel you can move things around easily and even give your left-brain a hand with the occasional bit of math.

So you don't have to flip back to a previous page, here is my one-year vision.

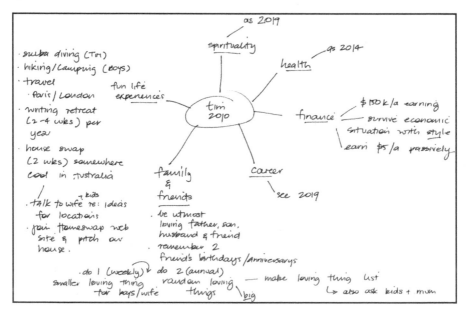

Trying to imagine the whole map in Excel can be a little daunting. So let's un-complicate matters and start with the Finance part for now. We'll get to the rest later. Here's how it looks:

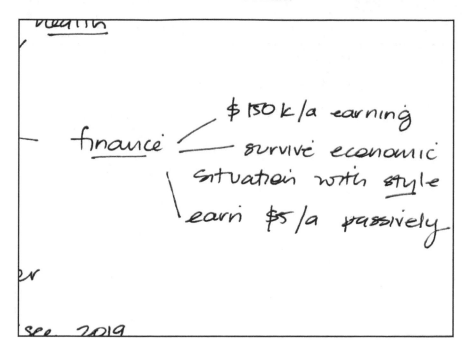

How to Excel in Mind Mapping

In Excel, I put the main topic 'Finance' in my first column, listing the detail from the mind map in my second column. Easy, right? It looks like this.

Tim's Life Summit / By Topic	
TOPIC	DETAIL
Finance	Earn $150k per annum
	Survive economic situation with style
	Earn $5k per annum from passive investments

And now I work it through, topic by topic, listing everything in the entire plan. I just work my way around the Mind Map. It ultimately looks like this.

TOPIC	DETAIL	FURTHER DETAIL

Tim's Life Summit / By Topic

TOPIC	DETAIL	FURTHER DETAIL
Finance	Earn $150k per annum	
	Survive economic situation with style	
	Earn $5k per annum from passive investments	
Career	Exclusively doing stuff I love to do	Writing
		Commissioned work
		Executive Producing projects
		Television projects
		Albums
		Books / magazines / papers / blogs
		Film projects
	Working with Great People with	Integrity
		Honesty
		Fun
		Aligned
Family & Friends	Be utmost loving father	
	Be utmost close friend	
	Remember Birthdays / Anniversaries	Make list
		Enter into reminder type website
	Random Loving Things	Weekly
		Special Annual Thing
Fun life experiences	Scuba Diving	
	Hiking / Camping I	
	Hiking / Camping II	
	Travel Paris / London	
	Writing Retreat	
	House Swap	Join Home Swap Site
		Book Home Swap Holiday
		Take Home Swap Holiday
Health & Spirituality	Daily Practice	

Step #4 – Month-to-Month Mapping

So now I have everything from the mind map in Excel. Bravo. The next step is to convert this into a Month by Month plan. That means that we want to **assign each task to a specific month, creating a timeline for these desires.**

Start by going through each item and intuitively writing down a month next to it. Simply look at each desire and ask 'When would I like to do this?'

For example, it makes sense to do my Hiking in the summer months along with my Scuba diving. (I just love it when the water is warm!) On the other hand, it makes sense to 'Be the utmost loving father' *all year round*. I just can't imagine saying to my wife 'Sorry, it's April and I'm not scheduled for loving husband right now'. So I jot that one down as 'All'.

My topic-by-topic spreadsheet winds up looking like this:

Tim's Life Summit / By Topic With Month			
TOPIC	DETAIL	FURTHER DETAIL	FREQUENCY
Finance	Earn $150k per annum		All
	Survive economic situation with style		All
	Earn $5k per annum from passive investments		All
Career	Exclusively doing stuff I love to do	Writing	All
		Commissioned work	All
		Executive Producing projects	All
		Television projects	All
		Albums	All
		Books / magazines / papers / blogs	All
		Film projects	All
	Working with Great People with	Integrity	All
		Honesty	All
		Fun	All
		Aligned	All
Family & Friends	Be utmost loving father		Put into perfect week
	Be utmost close friend		Put into perfect week
	Remember Birthdays / Anniversaries	Make list	Now
		Enter into reminder type website	Now
	Random Loving Things	Weekly	Put into perfect week
		Special Annual Thing	All
Fun life experiences	Scuba Diving		December
	Hiking / Camping I		April holidays
	Hiking / Camping II		October holidays
			May / December
	Writing Retreat		
	House Swap	Join Home Swap Site	Now
		Book Home Swap Holiday	July
		Take Home Swap Holiday	Jan / 2010
Health & Spirituality	Daily Practice		Already in perfect week

Good. Now, with a smidge of moving, cutting and pasting, I wriggle this around into a calendar format instead of a topic by topic format. If you're cunning you can even set things up to let the computer do the sorting function on the 'timing' column. Here's how it looks, laid out month by month.

Tim's Life Summit / Month by Month

2009		
March	Career	Stuff I love to do + great people
	House Swap	Join Home Swap Site
	Remember Birthdays / Anniversaries	Make list
	Remember Birthdays / Anniversaries	Enter into reminder type website
April	Career	Stuff I love to do + great people
	Fun life experiences	Hiking / Camping I
May	Fun life experiences	Travel Paris / London
June	Career	Stuff I love to do + great people
July	Career	Stuff I love to do + great people
	House Swap	Book Home Swap Holiday
August	Career	Stuff I love to do + great people
	Family and Friends	New Baby!
	Family and Friends	Girl Birthday
September	Career	Stuff I love to do + great people
October	Career	Stuff I love to do + great people
	Fun life experiences	Hiking / Camping II
	Family and Friends	Boy Birthdays
November	Career	Stuff I love to do + great people
December	Career	Stuff I love to do + great people
	Fun life experiences	Writing Retreat
2010		
January	Career	Stuff I love to do + great people
	House Swap	Take Home Swap Holiday
February	Career	Stuff I love to do + great people
	Fun life experiences	Scuba Diving
March	Career	Stuff I love to do + great people
	Random Loving Things	Special Annual Thing
In Perfect Week		
	Health & Spirituality	Daily Practice
	Random Loving Things	Weekly
	Family & Friends	Be utmost loving father
	Family & Friends	Be utmost close friend

And of course, it's not a perfect match to the original spreadsheet. Some ideas 'bit' me as I was working and I made small changes as I went. In scientific terms it's called **'refining the plan'.** It's all part of the creative process and as such, to be encouraged!

So with a few nips, tucks, and tweaks, I've 'translated' my free-flowing, right-brain mind map into a year of left-brain perfection, laid out month by month, just waiting for the Law of Attraction to make it so.

We're going to jump from perfect months to perfect days. What happened to the perfect weeks? We'll build them out of your perfect day. Just wait and see...

Step #5 – A Map of Your Perfect Day

As far as I can tell, everyone knows that life is too short to live each day at anything less than your idea of perfection. And yet people manage to give away huge chunks of their life to sub-par jobs, less than ideal relationships, and 'plain vanilla' daily experiences.

This is not done willfully. A lot of people simply let their lives *happen to them*. They don't take the time to form their thoughts into the vision of a perfect life, down to the last granule. That's what the Life Summit is all about.

At this stage of the Summit game, we've already accomplished a lot that most people don't. We've mapped out ten-year, five-year, one-year, and month-to-month plans for an ideal life. All that hard work has given you the detail you need to summon the broad sweeps of your perfect life.

But it's still not enough. It's good to map out the broad sweeps, the big picture, and the month by month progression towards perfection...but wouldn't you rather live the perfect day *today*?

Of course you would! So don't wait. Instead, let's figure out what your perfect day looks like, moment by moment, hour by hour.

A Note on Perfection

So what *are* the things you love to do every day? How do you like to spend your time? How would your day look if you made a conscious plan to live each day, rather than simply let the time *happen to you*?

Now, let me be completely candid with you. I *love* working with the Law of Attraction, but I'm not a taskmaster or a perfectionist. So even though I have my ideal day up on my wall, I don't beat myself up or get stressed out if I don't live it exactly the way I've mapped it out. It's my ideal day, the day that works beautifully for me, bringing out the best in me and my life.

If circumstances change, I don't worry or stress, because worry and stress aren't part of my perfect day no matter what. Instead I *release the details*, watching the day unfold in its own true perfection via the Law of Attraction.

Mostly, with a vision of perfection in the back of my head and possibly visited in my morning meditation, I do get my ideal day. Sometimes I get a day that turns out even more perfect than my vision, manifested for me by the Law of Attraction as it responds to my vision in its implacable way. When that happens I just **update my vision of perfection** and pop it up on the wall to replace the old one.

Mapping a Perfect Weekday

First, take some time to brainstorm the kinds of things that might turn up in your perfect day. You may want to split this into your perfect working day and your perfect weekend day, since these days are, for most people, fundamentally different.

Take a moment here to invite your right-brain back into the room for some creative work. Give yourself a bit of time, a nice space, some snacks and a facilitator if you wish. Ideally, of course, you'll be doing this every day as part of your ongoing Life Summit process, so all these resources will be in place and standing by.

Every map starts with a bullseye. Write 'My Perfect Day' in the middle of a sheet of butcher's paper and start answering the question 'What sorts of things make up my perfect day?'

You might ask yourself questions like

- What were the top three days of my entire life and what happened in them?
- What were my top ten working life experiences and how did they go?
- When is the ideal time to get up?
- When is the ideal time to go to bed?
- How much time do I like to spend asleep?
- How much time do I like to spend mucking around?
- How much time do I like to spend working and on what kinds of things?
- What kind of things do I like to do in the mornings?
- What kinds of things do I like to do at night?

Here's where I started, focusing on a perfect working day.

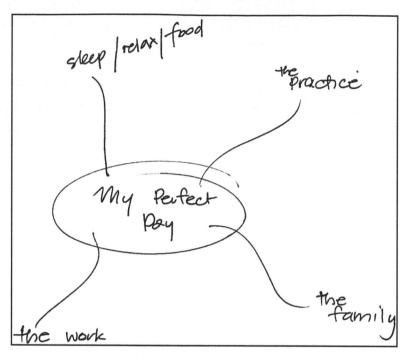

After sketching out the broad categories of my day, I start filling in the detail.

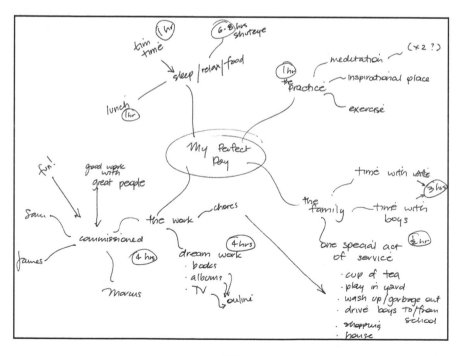

As you can see, I like to split my day roughly into working, sleeping and then the rest into family and relaxing time. (Those last two are frequently the same thing.)

I've also taken the time to make little notes of how long I'd like to spend on each. I have circled mine to make them stand out a bit.

I suggest you do this intuitively, asking 'how much time would I *like* to spend on this particular activity?' I certainly didn't do this with a calculator standing by, making sure it would add up. I just allowed myself to go with the flow and listen to my intuition a bit.

Okay then. You've got yourself a list of activity groups, each with the ideal amount of time. Now it's time to get myself back to the computer. Once I'm clear about what I'm going to write, plotting out the perfect day is a Word or Excel kind of task.

During this step, my left brain is behind the steering wheel and it insists that the activities in my day ultimately add up to 24 hours. So I enter the categories into Excel to check that out...letting it calculate the total number of hours for me. It looks like this.

The Timing of My Perfect Day		
Sleep / Relax / Food	Shuteye	7
	Tim Time	1
	Lunch	1
The Practice	Meditation + Exercise	1
The Family	Special Act	0.5
	Family Time	3
The Work	Dream Work	4
	Exec. Producing / Commissioned Work	4
Total Hours		21.5

As you can see, I actually have a few hours to spare, which I like. It sounds relaxed and stress-free to me to have a few hours of unidentified time each day. It sounds familiar, too, since a few unanticipated tasks invariably find themselves into my days...everything from a long call from a friend I haven't spoken to for a while to a quick trip to the vet to make sure the dog doesn't have fleas.

Amazingly the list on your Excel spreadsheet or in your Word doc is actually a minute-to-minute guide to your perfect day, just not in any particular order and not set against any particular time.

So I crank up Excel again and work these things in:

- a starting time
- a perfect order
- a finishing time

The great thing about using a computer for this is that you can always move things around, changing your mind as you go, until you have something that feels right.

Here's a simple 'map' in spreadsheet form, of my perfect day, one I aim to live every working day of my life.

My Perfect Day

7am	Shower / Shave / Up / Boys up
7:30am	**DAILY PRACTICE** Exercise / Meditate / Art
8am	
	1 hr
8:30am	Brekkie / drive boys to school
9am	**WORK** Story / Writing / Creative projects
10am	
11am	
	3 hrs
midday	Lunch break (meditate)
1pm	**WORK** Work for hire / Exec Producing / Meetings
2pm	
3pm	
	3 hrs
4pm	Communication / email / calls *1 hr*
5pm	Pick up boys from school / make dinner
6pm	Relax / Family Time
10 / 11 pm	Bedtime

As you can see, it's a pretty good match to my brainstorm. And, as I'm sure you might imagine, it did not spring to life fully formed. It has evolved over time and with changing circumstances...and will undoubtedly continue to do so.

Now, this list is pretty bare bones on the face of things. So let's talk about some of the items in greater detail so you can see how a perfect day looks in real life...*my* real life...

- **7 a.m.** - I'm up...whether I want to be or not (Having two young children in the family doesn't leave me much choice.)

- **7:30 a.m.** - My daily practice in the mornings gets me in the best possible frame of mind for the day. For me, this means exercise and meditation. On a sunny day, I go for a run otherwise it's Nintendo Wii Fit.

  My meditation, as detailed earlier in the book, is critical. It's my way of connecting with my spiritual side, bringing a higher inspiration into my day. It's in meditation that I frequently find out about amazing lateral new ideas to work into my day. It's also when I take the time every day to dwell upon the various details of my perfect life, without getting attached to the implementation aspects too much.

  Sometimes I just don't feel like doing any of that, which is fine also!

- **8:30 a.m.** - When I drive the boys to school, we play the game of talking about our intentions for the day. What kind of day is it going to be? While this is really just a fun game that the boys love, it's also a cue to the Law of Attraction to start organizing those kinds of things.

- **9:00 a.m.** - I usually have one thing in particular that I wish to focus on of a morning, since that's my prime time. I'm most focused and most productive in the mornings. I don't fight it, I just go with it, making the most of that time, knowing that things tend to slow down in the afternoon.

- **Midday** - is lunchtime around here, although if it strikes a little earlier or later, that's OK. I like to get out of my head at lunch.

- **1 p.m.** - I'm into my second block of work for the day. This is where I respond to the various pressures of the day. If I need to take meetings either at the office or away, I aim to do that in this block, where it won't disturb the most important things in my day.

- **4 p.m.** - I tend not to answer the phone or check my email during the day, preferring to keep my focus going. Instead, I defer these things to a single block at the end of the day, where I return all calls, check and respond to emails and faxes.

- **5 p.m.** - Finally, if I can, I finish at 5 p.m. When I'm busy, of course, this doesn't happen, but mainly it does. My family is pretty good about spending time together. We make dinner together, eat dinner together and generally hang out.

- **7 p.m.** - My kids go to bed, I spend time with my wife, and I hit the sack at around 10 or 11 p.m.

And that's my perfect day. Now that I've taken the time to clarify what an ideal 24-hour period looks like to me, it's amazing how often events conspire to help me live it perfectly.

So let's get started mapping out a perfect day for you...

Mapping the Perfect Weekend Day

At this point, I should be able to leave you to your own devices to map out your perfect weekend day. Just work the same process as the perfect working day, only leave out the work and replace it with play! There is no shortage of things to do in your weekend; I'm sure you know your own. Leisure time is one of the few things that most people are totally clear about.

Just make sure it adds up to roughly 48 hours of perfect weekend and you're there.

To be honest, I don't really plan my weekends that much. Our weekends are fairly organic. What I *do* do, however, is a quick meditation first thing Saturday morning or last thing Friday night to dream up some cool things for the weekend in front of me. I know this sounds pretty extreme but most Saturday mornings see me writing a quick list of the things that have popped, inspired, into my head while I'm having a shower. These are enjoyable things, adventures for me and the boys or the entire family.

Step #6 - Turning Days Into A Week

Now that you know what your perfect working day and perfect weekend looks like, your perfect week pretty much falls into place... just as I promised at the end of the last section. It's just 5 days of your perfect weekday and 2 days of your perfect weekend day. Easy!

With that in mind, here's *my* perfect working week, all mapped out as an extrapolation of my perfect day, with a few more specifics thrown in as they came to me.

The Perfect Working Week

	Monday	Tuesday	Wednesday	Thursday	Friday
7am			Shower / Shave / Up / Boys up		
7:30am			DAILY PRACTICE — Exercise / Meditate / Art		
8am			1 hr		
8:30am			Brekkie / drive boys to school		
9am	Creating My Perfect Week		DREAM WORK — Story / Writing / Creative projects		
10am					
11am					
midday			3 hrs — Lunch break (meditate)		
1pm	Exec. Producing / Meetings	Client Work	COMMISSION WORK — Exec. Producing / Meetings	Client Work	Exec. Producing / Meetings
2pm					
3pm			3 hrs		
4pm	Communication / email / calls 1 hr	Communication / email / calls 1 hr	Communication / email / calls 1 hr	Communication / email / calls 1 hr	Communication / email / calls 1 hr
5pm			Pickup boys from school / make dinner		
6pm	Relax / Family Time / Do Random Loving Thing for Friends / Do Random Loving Thing for Family				
10 / 11 pm			Bedtime		

From Perfection to Inspired

Look at you! In a surprisingly short amount of time, you've created

- A ten year vision of your Perfect Life
- A five year vision of your Perfect Life
- A one year vision of your Perfect Life, and
- A month to month plan for your Perfect Life.

You also have

- A picture of your perfect weekday
- A picture of your perfect weekend day
- A picture of your perfect week.

The last little piece of the puzzle is to link those things together. And that happens first thing every Monday morning in a little half hour session.

Creating My Inspired Week

The best way to create the perfect week is to simply spend some time focusing on just that. This is a very Law of Attraction moment. This is when you take the time to think about, re-envision and experience your perfect week unfolding in your mind **before it happens in real life.** This is the consistent, focused and unambiguous thought we discussed at length in the first part of the book and have continued to touch.

You've come to the juncture where the rubber meets the road and all your mapping is distilled into a **weekly practice**. Think of this as a workout...a training session that keeps you in shape to reach perfection.

It's so important...so valuable...so powerful...and yet **all it takes is 30 minutes.** So what specifically might you do in this half hour?

The short answer is, of course, *do anything* that puts your focus on what you desire. To be more specific, why not focus on the careful plans you've been working on that deliver, over the course of time, the life of your dreams?

You could start your weekly Life Summit 'workout' by grabbing your various plans and give them a good look through. Remember, these are working pages, so feel free to add stuff, remove stuff that is no longer relevant and add detail as it emerges. These should be working, living plans, so make them work and live for you! A little felt-tip pen action is all it takes.

If you have a facilitator or friend following this process with you, this is the time to give them that **weekly call**. I suggest that you keep the call informal, catching up on life and sneaking in some Life Summit gossip as you go. Nothing too structured or left-brain.

Certainly take time in that call or on your own to **state your intentions for the week**. What days of the week are you looking forward to? Where is your week looking a bit average, and what can you do to make those times above-average? What extra thing could you do, what little special treat could you add to your week to nudge it from being a good week to being a great one?

Next, work backwards and take a moment to visit the month by month plan you created in Excel. Again, this is a living, working document, so feel free to make changes as you go.

Then, with clarity about what you desire for the month (from your monthly plan), ask yourself a question: 'Which parts do I feel inspired to act on this week?'

Remember, if you're not sure which monthly plans to act on, take a moment to check in with your intuition. *How do you feel?* If, as you read one of your monthly line items, you feel you'd love to do it, go ahead and add it into your weekly plan. If you don't feel inspired to do it, then it's a sure sign you shouldn't be doing it *right now*. It's time will come later.

Warning! Warning! Warning! If there's nothing on your monthly plan that you want to do, then you need to revisit the Life Summit process because *everything in it should be something you want to do!*

The foundational question at the core of your Life Summit vision is, 'What is your perfect life?' Anything that is not part of your picture of perfection should not appear in any map or on any plan. If the answer to the question has changed since you did the process, then you can do without it. Instead, take a moment to come up with something else that you desire.

Make a note of the things from your monthly plan that you intend to do this week and, if you're a diary kind of person, book them in. I like **booking things into my diary,** which I keep on my PC in Outlook, since once they're booked I can forget about them until the designated time.

That's it! In half an hour you should be able to revisit your perfect week, tailoring it to be your best week ever, including the relevant inspired actions month by month from your perfect life plan. Once you're good at it you'll probably do it in ten.

Believe it or not, you've now completed all but the last, and I might say 'never-ending' part of The Life Summit process. It's time now to **live what you've created**. Until you start 'doing' Life Summit activities in your day-to-day existence, your desires will continue to elude you.

Living Life at the Summit

So here you are, your left and right brains in alignment, your whole being committed to creating visions of the perfect life that the Law of Attraction will manifest for you.

But what if you're having trouble and need a little help getting through some of the blocks that come up on the way? Read on ...

Troubleshooting the Life Summit Process

Of course, not everyone has an effortless, easy time of their first Life Summit. There's no question that the Life Summit process should delve deeply into the heart of your desires and this can be a difficult thing.

Here, then, are some examples of what I mean from recent Life Summits that I've facilitated professionally. These are people you 'met' earlier in the introduction. These are their stories...their challenges...and their real life triumphs with the Life Summit.

The Desire Block

Dean is an internet coding and design professional living in America. We spent a day together working on his Life Summit chart. In our preliminary discussions, we'd agreed to focus on his business life although I'd suggested we round out his session with some basic personal details. (I've found that business lives and personal lives are always deeply interconnected.)

When Dean arrived, my home/office was already set up and ready to go. We had all the food, stationery and goodwill you could hope for to set the scene for mind mapping. We'd even taken a little time to meditate to bring us into a nice, peaceful place. The phone was off the hook and the day was going to be completely and totally devoted to nothing but the Life Summit process.

I started by asking 'So Dean, let's talk about your desires.'

Dean replied 'I'm going to have to stop you right there'

Huh? I was naturally curious as to why Dean shut down so completely on the subject of what he wanted in life, so I asked him to explain things to me. It turned out that as a part of his pursuit of spiritual enlightenment, Dean had actually let go of all of his desires. Simply put, he'd become so enlightened already that he had no desires left.

Now *that's* what I call a block. My intuition told me I should accept his feelings on this and everything that came up that day. My intuition also told me that there was more here.

Rather than push against his position, which was perfectly reasonable in itself, I started to **flow around it**. This is a very Law of Attraction way to go. We explored what the spiritual journey meant for him. I asked for various details like when he'd started, how it felt and what it all meant.

It turned out that he'd started out on this path around ten years prior. I asked him whether he'd had any desires before then. It turned out that he had, of course. So instead of charting his desires ten years in the future, we did a comprehensive mind map of his desires from *ten years in the past*.

I'm not sure exactly when Dean had an 'Aha!' moment. While he'd locked all of his desires away behind his search for enlightenment, they weren't really gone. The Life Summit process can actually be quite cathartic in that way. As you talk about yourself for hours...even days on end...you discover things about yourself. You also re-discover things.

Dean re-discovered a lot. As we talked, he ended up filling a wall with his desires from ten years ago, finally realizing that they didn't exist only in the past. He still had desires for the here-and-now, and we worked together so he could use the Law of Attraction to achieve them.

The Left-Brain Block

Desiree is a mother, a wife and an extremely talented professional designer from London in the United Kingdom. Her husband is an executive in a top agency while she has taken the last few years off to bring up their little boy, Lee.

When Desiree came to me, she was on the cusp of getting back into her career and needed a little focus. From our brief initial conversations we knew she wanted to focus on business matters, but she was open to the process and understood that it would cross over from the professional to the personal.

As always, I had set up a space so that we could do a Life Summit, with food supplies, mapping supplies, and a big block of time that could be devoted to the process.

I explained to Desiree that we'd start by outlining then detailing a vision of her future ten years from now. But as soon as we began, I saw straight away that Desiree was a bit fidgety. She was finding it hard to focus and clearly had some kind of block.

When you're facilitating a Life Summit session it pays to clear up these kinds of things as soon as they come up. So I asked her what the problem was. It turned out that Desiree was getting agitated because she wanted to make sure, as this was a professional and therefore paid session, that we were going to cover everything she had in mind in the time we had available.

Intruder alert! Her left brain was clearly still in the room!

So we took a few minutes to outline, in mind map form, exactly what her desires were for our day of Life Summiting. One thing she brought up was a desire for clarity on an upcoming Christmas card printing project, for example. And a desire to clarify all her business projects, in fact. Once we'd written these and other desires up no the wall, Desiree relaxed.

Then, I actually opened the office door and asked her to let her left brain leave! Once that was done, I knew we were finally able to get down to business...or so I thought.

The Parent Block

Poor Desiree. As we got going on Step #1 ... clarifying her vision of her perfect life in 10 years ... it was clear that she was being blocked by more than just her left-brain.

At first, Desiree relaxed into the couch and started to outline her vision of a perfect life ten years in the future. She was terrific. Her vision was delightful and her imagination really flowed. She spoke about a perfect house with a huge yard. The garden was so big that she could feed her entire family with home grown vegetables. She would spend at least half an hour each day out there with her hands in the soil.

Desiree spoke about her health, her physical body, and her key relationships with friends and family. She spoke about some important life experiences she wanted to have including personal adventures and long family trips around Europe.

When it came to her financial life and her career, however, I noticed that she was unable to be specific about her desires. She spoke in general terms only. While she could tell me, for example, that she wanted to work with really nice people, she couldn't tell me what she *actually wanted to do.*

It's not that unusual for people to be blocked around one part of their life or another. In Desiree's case I later found out that she'd been engaging professional counseling help on this issue for several years. At the time, however, all I knew was that despite her best intentions there was a section of her chart that was lacking specifics.

'How do you feel about money?' I asked, and 'How do you feel about your career?' She went a little pale, scrunched her face up uncomfortably and drew her knees up against her body. It was clearly the wrong question to ask!

In this way, facilitation can be a very intuitive process. While you know that you're probing for answers you sometimes have to be a bit lateral in your questioning. She thought about what I had asked for a while, but try as she might, she couldn't really tell me anything useful. She was clearly quite blocked here.

If you can't clear a roadblock, what do you do? Go around it? So instead of fighting with that block I went the other way. We started speaking about what she wanted to do *as a child*. People often have clarity when they look back to that part of their lives.

With Desiree, that turned out to be the key. It was amazing to watch her face light up, her color come back and her words pouring forth in an unstoppable torrent.

As she started to remember the details of a flourishing artistic career, however, she also started remembering the problems. Her **family had been set against her artistic aspirations.** Her parents, who are both accomplished doctors, were worried that she would never make any money doing art. They campaigned actively to stop her.

Desiree had been robbed of her desires at an early age. In the end we had to reach for a box of tissues as she wept quietly on my couch, overwhelmed as the specific memories flooded back.

Pain is often part of life, and that's why it can also show up in the Life Summit process. Invariably the process asks you to search deeply inside yourself and anything can come up. In Desiree's case we were able to move through it quite naturally, despite the pain it caused her. In fact I've yet to have any problems that didn't resolve themselves quite easily during the session.

But let me be clear. The Life Summit and a facilitator cannot do the job of a trained therapist. If your mind mapping process covers any psychological issue that is serious and impacting your life in a major way, I recommend that you consult a professional.

When Desiree left a few hours later she was on Cloud 9. Me, too, since it was so gratifying to watch her make her breakthoughs. We were able to unlock her memories and work our way through the problem areas. We went on to outline Desiree's perfect career and financial picture. It's a delight to watch it unfold together.

The Scarcity Block

It turns out there are really two ways to see the world. You either see it as a place of abundance or a place of scarcity.

If you see the world as an empire of plenty where there is enough to go around, then you're talking abundance. In an abundant world there is enough food, enough money, enough time, enough resources, enough sleep, enough play, enough fun, enough air, enough of everything for everyone...no matter how many of us there actually are. This is a friendly, happy world in which you can afford to take your time, to do your best. It's a world of generosity and plenty.

In this abundant world view, one person winning means another person can win, too. *Everyone* can be a winner, in fact.

If, on the other hand, you see reality the way so many people do -- as a harsh, dog-eat-dog world — then you're talking scarcity. In a scarce world, resources are finite and distributed unevenly between competing parties. In this scarce world, when one person wins, another must lose out. When one person gets a promotion, someone else is demoted. When one person gets enough to eat, someone else goes hungry.

Scarcity means for everything 'good' that happens there is a balancing 'bad'. People with this world view live in constant competition with everyone, even sometimes their own friends and family, fearful that they won't 'get theirs.'

During a Life Summit, it's critical that you understand how these different perspectives influence your experience of life and color your feelings about fulfilling your desires. If you believe in scarcity then everything you desire comes at the cost of someone else's desire. People who believe in scarcity tend to run into blocks like 'Is there enough money for me?' or 'Is there a great job for me?' or 'Are all the good men taken?'

If, instead, you believe in abundance, then your desires tend to flow. After all, when there's enough of everything for everyone, then surely there's enough for you!

An abundant world view is also helpful in the process of detachment. In a scarce world view, if events don't unfold according to your expectation, there can be a sense that 'I missed out on my one shot!' In an abundant world view there are many opportunities, one after the other. If you don't catch the first one, that's okay...no biggie. There will be plenty more.

In a world of abundance, if you don't get the raise you want that's OK. Your raise is going to come another way. If a certain thing doesn't happen the way you had thought it, it's because a different and better option is about to present itself. If you don't get the girl you want that's fine. There's an even more amazing partner about to come into your life, just out of your sight.

The Process of Unblocking

Whatever the block might be — scarcity, desire, or whatever — the answer is always to *go with it*, don't try to go through it. These blocks, I find, are always there for a solid and reasonable purpose and shouldn't be directly confronted. I find it best to simply flow around them, asking for lateral details or stepping over to an entirely separate section of the chart.

So if you find a block around money...talk about family. When you find a block around family...focus on health. Then, in the gentle fullness of time, you can start to tickle at the edges of the problem area, working back towards it intuitively.

It's good to work laterally and creatively on these things. You'll remember that when Dean was blocked around desire I asked him about his childhood desires. When Desiree was blocked around career, we moved onto where she was going to be living.

And don't be afraid to delve into personal issues when appropriate. During a mind mapping session with my client Miriam, we kept coming back to a block around *men*. She appeared to have strong negative feelings around men that constantly colored her chart and distracted her from her vision. It was only when we took the time to map out a chart on all the important men in her life that we found and unblocked her issues around her father and ex-husband.

Keeping It Confidential

All of the stories in the previous pages remind me that I must remind you that the Life Summit process can raise an issue of confidentiality. When you're doing the session on your own in the privacy of your own home, of course, you're fine. No one is there to tell your innermost secrets to the world.

I would recommend, however, that you take your mind maps off the wall as soon as you're done. I once left one of my own, personal Life Summit sessions up by mistake. A naturally curious client came into my office several days later while I was making tea and innocently read the whole thing. Busted! I was in the awkward position of having to explain some of the right-brain craziness that was up there. Was *my* face red! Especially since this client hadn't yet done a Life Summit.

So if you have secrets, be sure to keep your charts private!

Accidental exposure is one thing. But the issue of confidentiality is really more likely to come up when you're working with a facilitator.

When you're working with a doctor or a lawyer, they are bound by doctor-patient and attorney-client 'privilege.' This is a legal term which says professionals are not permitted to disclose personal information about their patients or clients. In the corporate world, if items under discussion are confidential, you often sign a Non Disclosure Agreement or N.D.A.

In the practice of the Life Summit process, it comes down to trust. If you have a friend or family member working with you then you're probably okay because these are people you know and trust personally. When I'm working with clients, there's a level of professional trust. On the odd occasion when more is required, I generally make up some kind of confidentiality agreement right there on the spot which we both sign.

One way or another, it's best to **make a conscious effort to keep the private details private.** It's also a good thing to address *before* you start the process.

Some Final Thoughts

When I was in my early twenties my family started to get interested in having psychic readings. We weren't interested in the kind of reading you get in the freak-show alley at the circus. Instead we found a terrific intuitive medium called Bruce who went on to become quite famous through his books and television career.

Bruce had a way of connecting with something quite spiritual and profound. His sessions left you feeling like he knew you more intimately that you knew yourself.

Before he started, however, he needed to touch something personal. In my case he would hold my watch, eyes closed, while he searched for his connection.

The Life Summit process is a little like that watch. It brings up the most amazing and profound things. Even when you're not a professional medium like Bruce.

These 'Aha!' moments, wherever they come from, can be exhilarating and wonderful or profoundly upsetting. There can be tears of pain and weeping with uncontrollable joy within moments of each other. A lot of people talk about feeling emotionally wrung out after a Life Summit session because of this.

Simply put, the truth is *exhausting*!

There's something inexplicable that happens during a Life Summit session. The Life Summit process delves deeply into your inner life. It is designed to search out and discover your deepest desires. After all it is when you bring your deepest desires to light that your most perfect life can be lived. And isn't that what we're all here for?

Along the way, however, as there was with Bruce, there can be a connection to … the beyond. In my experience the Life Summit process routinely connects you to something else, to **something bigger than you.** This enlightened perspective, wherever it comes from, will tease itself into the cracks and spaces between your thoughts, inspiring your words and questions as you go.

Of course there's no need to look for it or search it out. It will happen naturally, on its own. It will find its own rhythm. Your only job, as with the rest of the process, is to *go with it.*

So when your facilitator asks you an off-the-wall question, just answer it! Don't think too much. Or if, as a facilitator, you're moved to ask something that looks totally unrelated, just ask it!

The Law of Attraction, after all, is working here too, answering your desire to experience the perfect Life Summit! So be sure to bring that intention, even in the back of your mind, into your session right from the start.

What to Expect when You're Expecting

Once you've done the Life Summit process you're going to expect to see results. And why wouldn't you? After all, that's the very reason that you took the time to do the process in the first place!

So let's have a look at the kinds of things that might unfold in the first hours, days and weeks after you've completed the Life Summit process.

The Morning After

Most people, having done the Life Summit process, feel quite **exhausted**. I recommend that you take the rest of the day off if possible, spending your afternoon quietly and peacefully. The best thing is to doze off under a blanket somewhere without thinking about it too much. Give your insights a little time to settle in on their own.

The process can also bring out **feelings of fear**. Some people, having seen what their perfect life looks like, can get quite upset. Now that they know what they *could* be doing they feel that they *should* be doing it. They feel the weight of their desires bearing down upon them.

This, of course, is completely unnecessary. If you feel like that, I recommend putting the Life Summit mind maps in a drawer for a few months. If they're terribly unsettling, then I recommend burying them in the back yard and hoping that they'll decompose before you feel like digging them up.

This is meant to be fun, remember? So if you're feeling all too serious about it, then simply put, **you're doing it wrong.** If you're feeling anxious, stop and think about your Life Summit maps for a moment. Searching for the things that actually *feel great*. Use your desires to quiet your fear and bring yourself back to that positive place.

Do you remember the emotional compass we spoke about before? Instead of heading towards fear, reorient yourself. Focus your mind on things that bring you to **a ten out of ten** for happiness.

The Illusion of Control

The other thing that people appear to confuse upon finishing their Life Summit is that it might put them in a position of control. They appear to believe that the level of clarity and detail brought up during the process means that they're in a position to 'make it happen.'

If you've been paying attention, *you* know this is wrong-headed thinking. The important thing is to remember that controlling your future is not your job. Your job is to get clear on what you want and then, simply, to let go. This doesn't mean that you're detaching yourself from your desires. It doesn't mean that you're not meant to care about your desires manifesting in the physical world or that you're not meant to enjoy it when they do. It means that you release the expectation that things will unfold in the specific configuration that you're imagining. In fact, endlessly screening the details of how your desires are going to unfold in your mind, like a mouse in a wheel, will just stress you out.

Instead, release that manifestation to a higher power. The Law of Attraction will bring these things to you. Your only job is to receive. You get to watch the details unfold with joy and laughter. Your job is to get better and better at recognizing the Law of Attraction when it's working for you. Keep an eye out for inspired thoughts, new ideas and connections as your day goes by. And when they feel *terrific* – then act on them!

After The Life Summit

In the days and weeks following your Life Summit, it will be tempting to try and chase down examples of the Law of Attraction working for you. I'm not a mad fan of this kind of behaviour. It sounds kind of stressful, don't you agree? Kind of like a dog running after a car. Instead, I recommend that you be a 'watcher' rather than a do-er. Just observe everything unfolding on its own.

Whether you choose to follow my advice or not about 'chill-axing' for a few days, however, don't be surprised if you have a tumultuous first week. The Law of Attraction can start working incredibly quickly.

Let's talk about what happens once you've had that nice nap on the couch. Most likely you're going to want to talk with your friends and family about what you've discovered in your chart. This makes a great deal of sense and lines up beautifully with the Law of Attraction because you're **making your thoughts into words.** Remember the section on 'thought, word and deed'? Well talking to your friends is all about the words.

Quite often, when you're talking the whole thing through over coffee with your friends, they can catch your excitement and start offering ideas. Terrific! Here the Law of Attraction is working like a charm, bringing new ideas and connections into your life. Write those suggestions down and put them in a draw, however, for a day or so.

The problem is that quite often your friends, having not been a part of the Life Summit itself, are not possessed of all the facts. As a result, they may start tuning in to what *they* want for you as opposed to what *you* want for you. So re-examine the ideas, thoughts, and helpful suggestions that you are given one by one and ask yourself, 'How does this idea, one of many suggested by my loving friends and family, feel?'

If it feels good, then act on it. If it doesn't resonate right now, then throw it back into the draw for later.

Stay In Touch with Your Intuition

Now let's say that it's a few days or maybe a week later. Quite often the ideas in your Life Summit have had a chance to settle. If there's anything that feels wrong, then throw it out. Just stop thinking about it, removing it gently from your thoughts. The things that are still swimming into your mind, like little minnows refusing to be ignored, are probably the right thoughts to focus on *as long as they feel good!* If you're going into fear and stress then you're doing the wrong thing. Try meditating to clear your mind and release any negative thoughts.

In the meantime you're most likely going to see things start to shift and move *on their own.* Again, your job is to identify your desires. The Law of Attraction will sort out the details of how it happens.

A lot of people report major changes in the days, weeks and months following their Life Summit. It's not unusual to hear about career changes, relationship changes, financial changes and even health changes. Again, there's no use in *trying* to make these happen. Your job is to stay focused on the desire itself, releasing the actual life experience to manifest in its own way.

Pay attention to your feelings. If you're inspired to act, then go for it. If you're not, then just sit with it for a while until you are. And if you're still not feeling inspired, then don't act! It's simple, right? And yet it's amazing how many people don't actually do this. So please pay attention to how you're feeling. Like anything, you'll get better with practice, so bring your feelings into your consciousness again and again. Ultimately it will become habit and then intuition to keep asking 'How do I feel about this?' as you decide again and again *what you're inspired to do in this new, unfolding moment.*

And again, if nothing happens, then that's OK too! Just practice getting clear on your desires and release your expectations. When things start to happen, you'll know.

What Do I Do Now?!

Once you've read the last page in this book and made your way through the six steps of the Life Summit, the real 'work' begins. Choosing your thoughts and actions so that they align with the Law of Attraction is a way of life...and in that way The Life Summit will continue to enrich your time on this planet forever. It's not something you can tick off your list and consider done forever.

With that in mind, we've created a web site intended as a great place from which to continue your Life Summit journey.

Before We Say Good-Bye

What's important to remember as you set out to embrace your perfect life is that the Life Summit is *a process*. It's not over when you turn the last page of this book; it's just starting. Living this process and therefore focusing on bringing the life you desire into being by means of the Law of Attraction is a constant thing. It's a lifestyle choice, really, surrendering your desires to a higher power in every moment.

From the outside it can look very difficult and highly risky. After all, asking yourself to *stop* trying to obsessively control your life can sound crazy and feel scary.

So ask yourself

- 'How well has trying to control my life, down to the minute details, worked for me up until now?', and

- 'Am I really in control or is that just something I like to think?', and then
- 'Maybe it would be good to try another way for a while'.

Give surrender a try and see how it goes for you. If it works for you, that's great. If it doesn't work, then you can always go back to obsessively trying to control your life.

Practice Makes Perfect

I would also like to point out that it's going to take a little while to learn how to do this and do it well. Like driving a car or any other worthwhile skill, it's going to take some practice until you really get it right. Along the way there you might struggle as you try to unlock the secrets hidden inside yourself. What are *your* greatest desires? What do *you* want for your life? These eternal questions aren't answered in a day.

With that in mind, I re-do to the Life Summit envisioning process every three to six months. And why do the process so often? Because your answers will change as your life unfolds. That's what the journey is all about!

A Desire to Give

Over the years, as I've facilitated this process, I've found that a lot of people are very *physically focused*. They desire *physical objects* like cars, houses and money and that's terrific! It makes sense.

I've also found, however, that there are some people who focus beyond themselves. These are people who are asking 'What can I give?' and 'How can I help?' This sort of focus and these kinds of desires work incredibly well in creating a perfect life.

For example, when I used the Life Summit process to dream up my television show, I didn't ask for 'The best TV show in the world so that I can become rich and famous'. I asked, instead, 'To bring light, laughter and inspiration to the world'. It's a little corny, I know, but it expressed my desires nicely. In my experience, a **focus on *giving* instead of *getting* is in harmony with 'the Universe.'**

After all, it couldn't hurt to have a few million more people focusing on bringing world peace, solving world hunger and ending all disease, right?!

A Helping Hand

In addition to laying out a series of core concepts, tools and processes, this book has also covered some of the stumbling blocks during and immediately after the process. For every example that I've explored, however, there are dozens more. Hopefully I've covered the most common ones.

In the event that some are missing, however, please take the time to connect with our community directly online (at www.thelifesummit.com). That way you can bring your issues to light in a broader context and more people will benefit when we solve them together there.

Wrapping It Up with a Bow

The Life Summit process is going to work differently for every person. For some it brings amazing breakthroughs and instant results. For others it's a quieter, more contemplative experience.

The premise, however, is always the same. Focus unambiguously and consistently on what you want and it will come to you. The Life Summit process brings you that unambiguous and consistent focus. The Law of Attraction will take it from there.

It's been a great pleasure to write this book after working with this process for so many years. It's been my chance to share a powerful set of concepts, tools and processes with you.

It is *my* desire that the Life Summit process will deeply improve the lives of millions of people across the entire planet...including yours.

My thanks for your time and focus on this, with all my best hopes and intentions for you,

Tim

September 2009

A Note of Thanks

As you can imagine, 'translating' The Life Summit into book form has taken the time, effort, love and support of an enormous team of friends, family and colleagues.

So I'd like to send out a **huge thanks** to everyone who has been a part of this. And specifically, I'd like to make special mention of:

- ☐ All my amazing Facebook friends who have offered comment, feedback and support the whole way through
- ☐ All my Life Summit clients who have kindly agreed to let me publish their stories
- ☐ The folks at Morgan James, especially David Hancock, my liaison Lyza, and the whole EVM team
- ☐ My core manuscript team including my editor Debbie Feldstein at Creative Blocks and my parents Anita and Chris
- ☐ My BFFs Derek, Joseph and Dune and of course, the amazing Maria

To each and every one of you, I can say without hesitation: you're all amazing!

And of course, all of my love and appreciation go to my wonderful (and understanding) family: my lovely wife Angela, our sons Zak and Finn and our beautiful new daughter Isabella Scarlet. *You* are my perfect life.

And lastly, let me conclude with an acknowledgement that this work has been inspired, which is to say co-created, with Spirit that allowed things to flow naturally and to bring me to this place.

What a wonderful way to work!

Free Extras Online

As you might have noticed on the front cover of this book, there is an ever growing library of BONUS MATERIAL available online. My intention over the coming months is to stockpile a mountain of useful videos, audios, and written resource material that you can access at-will, whenever you wish.

As you can imagine, there's lots more to talk about when it comes to The Life Summit and the Law of Attraction than could possibly go into a single book. Those extra chapters will be published online, one month at a time.

Your go-to online resource will offer 'hot' topics like these:

Not Fighting with your Wife
- Clarity
- Not Feeling Lost
- Snoring
- The Opposite of Fear

The information is substantive, but the style is light and easy. I hope you will use it to bring some fresh inspiration to your day. You can download them whenever you're ready and bit by bit, you'll create your own Life Summit library.

Simply go to the web site www.thelifesummit.com and click on 'FREE STUFF.'

The instructions for the password are online because they're going to change from time to time. They will always be based a certain word from a certain line from a certain page in the book.

It's that easy!

BUY A SHARE OF THE FUTURE IN YOUR COMMUNITY

These certificates make great holiday, graduation and birthday gifts that can be personalized with the recipient's name. The cost of one S.H.A.R.E. or one square foot is $54.17. The personalized certificate is suitable for framing and will state the number of shares purchased and the amount of each share, as well as the recipient's name. The home that you participate in "building" will last for many years and will continue to grow in value.

Here is a sample SHARE certificate:

HABITAT FOR HUMANITY

THIS CERTIFIES THAT

YOUR NAME HERE

HAS INVESTED IN A HOME FOR A DESERVING FAMILY

1985-2005

TWENTY YEARS OF BUILDING FUTURES IN OUR COMMUNITY ONE HOME AT A TIME

1200 SQUARE FOOT HOUSE @ $65,000 = $54.17 PER SQUARE FOOT
This certificate represents a tax deductible donation. It has no cash value.

YES, I WOULD LIKE TO HELP!

I support the work that Habitat for Humanity does and I want to be part of the excitement! As a donor, I will receive periodic updates on your construction activities but, more importantly, I know my gift will help a family in our community realize the dream of homeownership. **I would like to SHARE in your efforts against substandard housing in my community!** *(Please print below)*

PLEASE SEND ME _____ SHARES at $54.17 EACH – $ $_____

In Honor Of: _____

Occasion: (Circle One)   HOLIDAY   BIRTHDAY   ANNIVERSARY

        OTHER: _____

Address of Recipient: _____

Gift From: _____ *Donor Address:* _____

Donor Email: _____

I AM ENCLOSING A CHECK FOR $ $_____ PAYABLE TO HABITAT FOR HUMANITY OR PLEASE CHARGE MY VISA OR MASTERCARD *(CIRCLE ONE)*

Card Number _____ Expiration Date: _____

Name as it appears on Credit Card _____ Charge Amount $ _____

Signature _____

Billing Address _____

Telephone # Day _____ Eve _____

PLEASE NOTE: Your contribution is tax-deductible to the fullest extent allowed by law.
Habitat for Humanity • P.O. Box 1443 • Newport News, VA 23601 • 757-596-5553
www.HelpHabitatforHumanity.org

Printed in the USA
CPSIA information can be obtained
at www.ICGtesting.com
JSHW082206140824
68134JS00014B/453

9 781600 376948